Healing Energies

Second Edition

A system of preventing disease by studying the blueprint of the body.

by
Dr. Stephen Paul Shepard

Foreword by Stevan Cordas, D.O., FAPM
Past President of the International
Academy of Preventive Medicine

Second Edition
1st printing Oct. 1983

BiWorld Publishers
P.O. Box 62
Provo, Utah

Acknowledgements

Thanks to Betty Gay for typing this manuscript, and to Ty Harper for the illustrations and art.

Thanks to Dr. Dan Farmer and Dr. John Sawtelle for assistance with proof-reading.

Notice to the Reader

DEDICATED TO
MY WIFE AND FRIEND

Table of Contents

Section I

FOREWORD

T he fact that some form of biologic energy is involved in human disease and health has been appreciated in many cultures in the past. Unfortunately, this concept is now shrouded in mystery and is not appreciated by the modern scientific medical community. With the advent, however, of new field theory physics, initiated by Bohr, Einstein, Plank and others, an entirely new appreciation of the link between energy and matter has occurred in the past one hundred years.

The life force that animates man is the essence of the energy that I am referring to. What sustains the life force in man? How can we measure it? How can we increase it? Does it, in essence, control our destiny, longevity and health? Of course all of these questions cannot be answered scientifically at this time, but all of us can appreciate this animating life force and its major expression in man-consciousness. The study of energy at the most subtle levels is in the province of physics, while the study of consciousness is a portion of the study of psychology. The training between these two disciplines is diverse enough so only a few gifted and prophetic writers, such as Kafka, Ornstein, Burr, Hill and Tiller have, in modern times, explored the relationship of the two sciences and attempted to objectify, where possible, the human energy systems. Twenty-five years from now it should be possible, using delicate magnetometers specifically designed to detect human radiation, to diagnose and modulate disease patterns in humans. Such work currently is being done, but is largely in an investigational stage. The pendulums, radionic machines, color machines and similar devices used in the past have not gained acceptance and are unlikely to do so in the future, no matter what their validity may be in experienced hands. Our science is trapped into a principle that requires double blind studies, laboratory experiments under controlled conditions. This principle will retard the eventual scientific investigation of the biologic energy system of man. However, it will not totally inhibit this discovery, for as our investigations grow with the surge of neo-Einsteinian physics and its modifications as a basis, many feel that Albert Szent Gyorgi's plea for basic scientists to recognize and investigate the micro electrical state in man will be answered. Within man there is a complex electrical system headed by a computer greater than Xerox and IBM put together, with each cell being a micro transformer/capacitor and even a rudimentary memory chip. Conversion from sensory to electrical to chemical energy is in itself amazing, but the communication of the organism as a whole, in its relationship to its environment, is even more so. Dr. Shepard has done an excellent job of exploring an area of the body's energy system.

His book will describe a method of surface magnetic exploration that allows a nontechnically trained person to gain information about his health needs or those of his family. It does not represent all aspects of the life force or the varied potential energy systems involved in man, but merely that portion dealing with certain reflexes that appear to work magnetically and allow the computer within man to provide the necessary information. A technically oriented individual may wish to read the chapter provided for the physician so he can tune himself more objectively to the author's goals and objectives. For the physician reader, it is suggested that he read the section provided for him first in the appendix. This method has been called SK (Screening Kinesiology). Dr. Shepard refers to it as myonutritional testing.

The artist has provided helpful illustrations and additionally provides two characters throughout the book: The dragon representing illness and other character representing "You".

Steven Cordas, D.O., FAPM

Is it more than just nerves?
What's eating you?

Section II

THE BODY IS A MAGNET

Betty F. entered my office with a complaint of tiredness, recurrent headaches and periods of weakness and confusion during the day. She told me that sometimes she gets very mixed up and becomes more depressed and anxious over her inability to accomplish the things in life that she would like to do, her declining libido and the family problems that were occurring as a part of her illness. She had been this way for two and a half years, and told me that another physician had done a glucose tolerance test which was reported as being normal, but she had a suspicion that she had low blood sugar anyway. Hypoglycemia, or low blood sugar was discussed with her by the other doctor, who "didn't believe in it" and supplements were felt not to be necessary "if she ate a reasonable, well balanced, American diet." In listening to her history, I felt it was possible for her glands or nervous system to be out of tune and I respect the fact that probably all of us could have low blood sugar tendencies from time to time, depending on the type of stress that we are facing and the natural resistance provided by our parents to begin with.

I took a standard history and physical and followed that by some blood testing and a glucose tolerance test over five hours,

5

which was preceded by a diet, for several days, of rich refined carbohydrate-type foods. I don't use glucose tolerance tests now as often as I used to, for reasons that I will discuss later, but in her case, there was a distant history of diabetes and the computer test showed an initial blood sugar of 130, which is a little bit high, and I was interested in finding out if she was diabetic and coincidentally if she had a very rapid fall in her blood sugar. In fact, she was, and the blood sugar rose to 190 in the first hour, 220 in the second hour and rapidly fell to 60 in the third hour. It was during this time that she became confused, shaky and weak. The patient did have a reactive type of hypoglycemia with not enough sugar reaching the brain rather suddenly, resulting in confusion. There was also a release of adrenalin characteristic of a sudden stress on the system which resulted in nervousness, shakiness, paleness and cold sweat. Yet the blood sugar never went below 60 and studying the other doctor's report, we found that he had done a three hour sugar test, did not give her a special diet for two or three days before the glucose tolerance test, and in fact, she was hospitalized at that time and lying around in the hospital. We know that a glucose tolerance test will change its character in an artificial setting and officially must have a special diet preceding the test for several days and should be carried out for five hours if you are also looking for hypoglycemia. Hypoglycemia may only be found in the fourth, fifth or even sixth hours, and thus not seen on the regular three hour test.

Since there has been a new classification of diabetes in the past year or so, the other physician took a liberal attitude that this patient didn't have diabetes at this point, but it is obvious to me that the pancreatic cells dealing with insulin were putting out the insulin in an abnormal way and she probably represented an early diabetic state. Blood insulin levels were not conducted in her case, because of the expense, but are useful in special cases and should be done right along with blood sugars.

Betty's case was discussed because she represents a common condition which has been termed psychophysiologic neuro-endocrine reaction by the new psychiatric coding, her abnormal nerve and glandular reaction results in this form of low blood sugar, probably compounded by a genetic tendency towards diabetes in her particular case. We feel that the term, however, is misleading because the psychophysiologic would indicate that the psychologic factors always precede the physiologic, and in fact, either event may occur and we may have a physiopsychologic dysfunction just as easily as we can have psychophysiologic one.

Betty's case is interesting also in that it represents a response to some type of stress, and the conclusion of her other physician, that she needed Valium tablets and was just anxious, was not correct in that he failed to specifically ask questions about the types of stress that she might be undergoing. It is sometimes easier to treat effects than to look for causes. In Betty's case, the stress was threefold. She had some conflicts with her husband and started to drink alcohol, probably in excess of her capacity to deal with it. Second, she had moved into a new home that was insecticided, and it was not appreciated that the insecticide itself might stress an already disturbed glandular or nervous system even more. Thirdly, she had sustained several bee bites, which seemed to increase her allergic symptoms from that point on, such as sinus trouble, nose congestion and coughing.

So, as we analyze her case, it is not unusual to see a complex individual with several types of stress occurring rather close to each other, who may have a continuation of symptoms, even though some of the original problems seem to subside. Another problem with the usual system of medicine is that the persistence of sickness after the initial trigger seems to subside or be corrected, is not well appreciated except in the case of infectious disease, which may leave a residue, or psychiatric disease, where there is an implied, abstract malefic force still going on that is not recognized by the patient because it is either subconscious or she is "hiding something".

Unfortunately, stress isn't that simple, and, as we will explore later in the book, comes in many ways and has to be respected as a cumulative response to a variety of different potential problem-causing factors rather than everything being psychiatric or toxic or infectious.

In studying Betty's genetics, we find that she has a diabetic and an allergic background. When these two backgrounds are combined, in my experiences, we often find that after the body begins to decompensate (not continue to be able to adjust to the different types of stress), perhaps because of a special "straw that broke the camel's back", the symptoms often persist and they become more sensitive to chemicals, foods, airborne factors, and often express it in the form of rapid drops in blood sugar, which may or may not be below critical levels as recognized by established medicine.

As I reviewed Betty's laboratory work, there were no major variations in the computer readout. I realize that a hair analysis might have revealed some problems, but that was not done on this patient, again for financial reasons. But, in addition to the usual lab tests and examinations which did not contribute a great deal of significant information, except to rule out major glandular failure or incidental liver or kidney disease or other signals of cancer or internal problems of that type, we proceeded with a reflex body mapping survey. Betty thought it was interesting, and I discussed the basic physical principle of what I was doing with her. Once the mystery of doing something new is eliminated, a majority of the patients will understand the advantages of these special reflexes and be very impressed with three important areas of the test.

First of all, it is inexpensive, and many doctors do it as a portion of the physical examination and do not charge extra for it. Secondly, there is no pain, needles or trauma involved in the tests. Lastly, it provides information that cannot otherwise be provided by history, physical examination or laboratory test, including a glucose tolerance test. Coincidentally, it provides information not available in a hair analysis except by inference.

The result of the test showed that Betty's adrenal gland, thyroid gland, and pancreas were not working up to par, that her stomach acid wasn't being produced properly at the time that she ate, that her calcium was low in relationship to magnesium, that she needed iron, in spite of a low normal serum iron on the blood test, and that she was needing more bioflavonoids and vitamin C.

Since I have done this test on several thousand individuals and have come to have faith in myself in reproducing the results, have faith in the tests per se, and have seen the results over a period of years produced in providing therapy guided by, in part, the tests and in part, the particular needs of the patient psychologically, socially and economically as well as physically, we proceeded with a nutritional program to assist this patient. The reason we chose nutritional factors, in spite of being licensed to use drugs, is because we do not know specifically of a helpful drug, other than amphetamines, that might cheat to quickly make her feel better. In the case of amphetamines, there is more harm than good, since they would aggravate the neurologic and glandular abnormalities after a short while.

Our goal was to restore a better autonomic or neurologic functioning as well as better glandular functioning. If we are producing less than adequate amounts of hormone, no matter what the blood test shows when compared with "normal" or average, the reflex will reveal it. The uniqueness of the reflex-magnetic testing is that it compares how your body is able to perform with what the brain computer perceives as the ideal thing to be done. If you don't match your ideal, the inner wisdom will tell you via this reflex. It was a jolt to me when I first learned that I could get the secret information and tap the mystery of the body by this simple a test.

We assisted Betty's thyroid, adrenal and pancreatic areas with glandular support. In the case of the adrenal, Cortisone was not used, but rather a dehormonized adrenal substance from beef. We calculated the vitamin C dosage, thyroid doses and the type of calcium specifically.

In essence, Betty was like a car who was out of tune, and we merely provided a fine retuning on the spot. By giving the basic building blocks, we are hopefully retuning and building rather than covering up and palliating. It gave us time to explore Betty's stress as it currently existed and to try to work out better choices and alternatives to let her express herself and allow her to build more confidence and rapport with me.

Betty was clinically better in all ways within seventy-two hours and required additional structural support, with manipulations and several detoxification techniques, as her level of general body toxicity was higher than it should have been, psychologic counseling and the appreciation that she was allergic or toxically sensitive to several grains, especially wheat, corn and cane in a refined form. Since these are basic ingredients that make up alcohol, this served to remain a severe stress to the system.

Betty was not an alcoholic as we currently would think of one, but she had enough problems with the grains that alcohol simply served as an extremely refined source of grain and she also had problems with several types of sugar, cornstarch, cornmeal and cornpaste as well as whole wheat and white bread. Certain changes were made in her diet accordingly, and after a period of time, using further nutritional support, she improved even more.

Betty's complete case was discussed so that the reader would not assume that merely learning the magnetic map and following the general directions of health care provided by listening to the body, was enough to automatically de-stress an individual. De-stressing is usually done by a professional, and many individuals who only take supplements of herbs will only feel better for a period of weeks or months, and if they don't get to their source of stress, will be discouraged with the partial answer provided. But, in addition to the three advantages mentioned above, this technique is a valuable health tool for both doctors, para-professionals and the lay public alike, because it is reproducible if all the rules are followed, gives insight to a deeper layer of healing than drugs can provide for, and in many cases where glandular deficiency or nutritional deficiency is the primary answer, will solve the problem automatically. It will also give you clues as to the source of stress in cases of mechanical and psychologic problems and can be used to help identify potential toxic stressors as well.

As more is learned to expand this map, undoubtedly revised editions of this book will have to be made, but even though the science and art from which it is originally derived, applied kinesiology, is an extremely complex and difficult area to master for even the skilled physician, this map was chosen because it is time to take the mystery out of the closet. I felt the current methods which had been presented to the lay public were still too complicated to be grasped by a majority of those interested.

This book is designed to teach the lay person (and the doctor) a method to help learn more about the patient than ever thought possible. It is based on Dr. Diamond's teaching.

A great deal can be learned from this method: More than blood tests and X-rays in many cases. Please, however, do not rely only on this system to gather information. No specific or exact disease can be diagnosed by it and no claims or cures can be made with it.

Remember, no one ever cures you but the God-given abilities inside you. No penicillin shot, no doctor, no friend—you are doing it. Don't look for the magic pill or shot. Drugs help to cover up the problem or deal with a part of it. At times, they give you the time to recover on your own.

This method which we will call muscle testing will, however, give you beautiful and accurate information that something is wrong inside before any blood tests are abnormal and even after they return to normal.*

The specific areas that are wrong are less important than interpreting *why* they are wrong. Many lay people could use the services of a nutritional or preventative medicine-oriented doctor at that point for better correlation. Doctors have many facts, statistics and skills to make sense of what you find and can double check your results, sometimes following up these test with X-rays or blood tests to look further. What we measure with the muscle test appears to be magnetic differences in certain spots on the body.

Since it contains electricity, *the body is a magnet*. This magnetic energy has been recently verified at a special laboratory

*Muscle testing or myonutritional testing is not the same as kinesiology or applied kinesiology.

at M.I.T. If the body is eighty percent water, and water is a good conductor of electricity, then it makes sense that we have a weak magnetic energy around us. We can measure the electrical energies using cardiograms, brainwaves or EMG's, but it is not yet possible for doctors to directly measure the small differences in the actual magnetic field around us.

Muscle testing was already established by physical therapists and arthritis specialists to see how strong the muscles were when a pioneering doctor from Detroit, began to put a puzzle together. Dr. George Goodhardt was this doctor and today, nearly thirty years later, is one of the true geniuses of this method which is called applied kinesiology.

What I am about to show you is a small part of this complicated system, but one that I think you can easily learn and use. It will show you if your main glands, nervous system, vitamins, minerals and organs are working up to par. Your nerves come from your brain (a complex computer greater than IBM and Xerox put together) and go to every cell in your body.

If your skin has a magnetic factor that is invisible, it has been shown that certain areas on the outside tell us about deeper layers on the inside. We feel that this information goes from the skin to the brain by way of special nerves (autonomics). Actually, we are looking at a blueprint of your body to guide us to what to do before actual physical sickness shows up. Of course, the reflexes will show a problem with true inner disease. That is why medical help may still be needed in some cases.

Some of you will not find a doctor around who will cooperate with you in understanding what you're doing. Unfortunately, you must decide what to do in these cases because no one can advise you of any specific disease or diagnosis accurately in the written word. We are all so different!

I will discuss some general ideas about these reflexes and natural things that can help in many cases. Sometimes there is more serious physical or mental disease, however, that cannot be taken care of without professional help.

In addition to the muscle testing to help you, I will give you some other tips to guide you in picking up problems.

Other books have been written about muscle testing, both for doctors and for lay people. They are generally complicated and involve many muscles to test. I was asked by many people to write this book due to the simplified method that I teach. Doctors who want to learn the more complicated system should take a 100 hour course offered by the International College of Applied Kinesiology.

A good introduction to this method that covers many other areas of this type of testng is written by John Diamond, M.D. "Your Body Doesn't Lie". Remember, some of these magnetic points on the skin were discovered by the Chinese and Indians thousands of years ago.

Section III

BASICS OF MUSCLE TESTING

L ike playing a piano or learning to type, you will get better with a little practice. It comes easier to some people than others.

Realize that you are measuring a very sophisticated system of biologic energy that is currently not provable by regular hospital testing. Other ways of measuring magnetic changes in the body are slowly gaining recognition, including magneto encephalography, magnetic blood flow techniques, magnetic ballistocardiography and nuclear magnetic resonance, to mention a few.

Have confidence that the future will verify that what you are doing is right. In fact, our *first* rule is to have confidence in yourself when you do the testing.

RULE TWO: Next, please remember to analyze the patient with the same attitude as you would have if you tune a radio or look at a thermometer. In other words, do not try to guess what the result will be ahead of time. Your bias attitude or wishes *can* influence the results. As long as you stay in a *neutral* mode, your results will be accurate and reproducible. Ask your patient to be *neutral* as well.

RULE THREE: Keep breathing in an ordinary way. The patient's test is influenced by a variety of external influences such as loud noises, bright lights, and even an abrupt change in your breathing. So, breathe easy and normal. Don't hold your breath at the time of a test.

RULE FOUR: Though usually you can still get an accurate test, to reduce problems with testing that can influence a few patients, have them take off their rings and watches and you take yours off as well. Since metal across the midline can also influence the test, it may be necessary to remove the patient's metal framed spectacles or dental bridge if the metal in the latter bridges across from the middle of the mouth.

RULE FIVE: Avoid loud music, especially any rock music, since certain rhythms can weaken the system. It is better to turn off any music at this stage of learning. Also, prevent any light from shining into the patient's eyes directly.

You are now ready to test the muscle. I usually use the left arm, extended directly out. The elbow must be straight. Place your left hand gently on the patient's right shoulder—this is to better balance yourself when testing the left arm. This also helps you detect if the patient raises the right shoulder to help himself (cheat) during the test. If he does, tell him not to do this, as it can influence the results. Now place your right hand gently on the back of the left wrist (right where the wristwatch would normally be). Without pressure, let your hand lie there for a brief moment, so that the patient can subconsciously get used to your temperature and "touch". Now, without a jerking motion, increase pressure with your right hand, *after* commanding the patient to resist. Apply enough pressure to check the strength of the left shoulder muscles (supraspinatous and deltoid) *without* forcing the arm down. This is the part that requires a little practice. You are *not* having a contest to see who is stronger. It is possible to even test children and weak adults with this method, if you realize you are testing the strength of their muscle, not yours. A lighter pressure is necessary in some patients than others. Pretend that you are the patient's muscle and wishing to be fully tested without overdoing it. Repeat the test twice so that

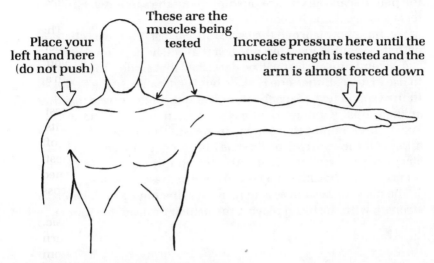

These are the
muscles being
tested

Place your
left hand here
(do not push)

Increase pressure here until the
muscle strength is tested and the
arm is almost forced down

Figure 1. MUSCLE TEST ONE

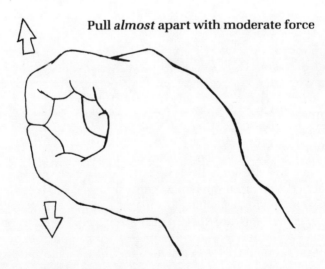

Pull *almost* apart with moderate force

Figure 2. MUSCLE TEST TWO

the patient can see you are pushing about the same. Ask him if he feels you are doing it about the same.

You have now learned the basic muscle test. This test is helpful with this method in all but one test that will be described later.

A second muscle test will be described that some people prefer to use instead. Either one is okay, but I generally use the first test. In the second test, place the thumb and the index finger together at their tips. (Opponens muscle). Now, try to pull the fingers apart, after telling the patient to resist. The same other rules apply. All the muscles of the body become a bit weaker when a stress happens to the body. We are simply using this phenomenon to our advantage by testing one of these muscles.

The nervous system acts to provide a fine tuning of the muscle strength with the brain playing the primary role in this tuning.

Section IV

FACE

1. Look at the face. Is it happy? Sad?
2. Is the forehead wide and high (intelligence) or narrow and low?
3. Are the lips full (caring, sensuous) or very thin (cold and calculating)?
4. Are the eyes dull or shiny?

Chinese and Japanese doctors attach much importance to the face and can tell about the physical and mental problems from it. We cannot go into greater detail with this, but will emphasize the face more than most areas.

TEST I: SWITCH CIRCUIT:

Hold your subject's left arm straight out—elbow straight and tell him to resist and test his muscle strength as described before. Do it again, but this time have him put the right hand, palm down, on the top of his head. Test the left arm again. Now, have him turn his hand over so that the back of his hand is on the top of his head. Test the left arm again.

INTERPRETATION: Since you are standing upon a great magnet, the earth, and your body is electromagnetic, there will be

19

a magnetic difference between the top of your head and the soles of your feet. This difference is also present on the front versus the back of your hand. Since the top of your head is north seeking (South Pole) and your palm is south seeking (North Pole), when you put these two together, there is an attraction and your body is not disturbed—your muscle (or your subject's) should remain strong. The back of the hand is north seeking (South Pole) just like the top of your head, so when these two are placed together, the strength in the indicator (left arm) muscle on testing will get weak instantly.* It is like putting two South Pole magnets together— they repel. In the case of the human body, the currents are too weak to feel this repulsion. The computer in your brain perceives it immediately as a micro-stress and momentarily, as an inner reflex to all the muscles, weakens your body a little. You are simply recording this weakness before and after testing. This is the normal response and is called a normal master or number one circuit. Remember, scientists tell us we are only using ten to fifteen percent of our brain, so the mysterious areas in the other eighty-five percent appear to have the powers to tell us the truth, including the accurate response to these circuits. All normal people will respond this way north of the equator. I don't know if it will change south of the equator, but probably not. The poles merely reverse.

What happens if the opposite reaction occurs and if you get weak when your left arm is tested and your right hand is placed palm down on the top of your head and if it gets strong when the right palm is placed palm up on the top of your head? It indicates a disturbed magnetic flow or flux (a switch) and indirectly reflects a poor healing energy. These people will have problems getting better. They are often toxic, anxious and get lost easily. They have trouble with remembering left and right, and often react adversely to drugs, foods, etc. They are chronically "allergic" and synthetics in the world are often adverse to them.

I call this my #1 switch circuit and if reversed, it must be corrected before you go on. To change this circuit, I recommend taking Ribonucleic acid (RNA).

*Some investigators feel that the reverse occurs in females but we have found the same reflex in both sexes.

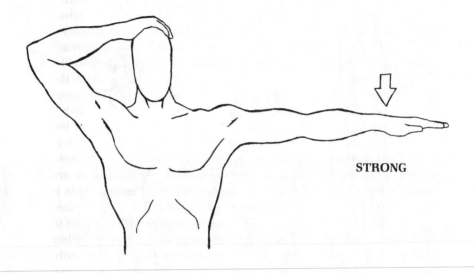

STRONG

TEST # 1. SWITCH CIRCUIT NORMAL REACTION

Ribonucleic acid tablets can be found in nutritionally oriented doctor's offices or some health stores. RNA is a complicated protein molecule that is essential to the life processes. DNA, its bigger brother, contains all of our genetic codes and lets us develop into who we are. RNA helps the DNA by "directing traffic", so to speak, and assists in the creation of enzymes, protein and other molecules. RNA tablets are normally of beef source. If you are allergic to beef, homeopathic RNA will also work. (Available from a doctor dealing with such formulas).

Sometimes a patient will stay strong no matter if he places the front or back of his hand on his head. Have him take his shoes off, as he may need to be better grounded. He will often then test satisfactorily. RNA will also cause this neutral reflex to change to a normal response. More than one RNA may be needed and it is better to bite into or chew the tablets. People using marijuana or

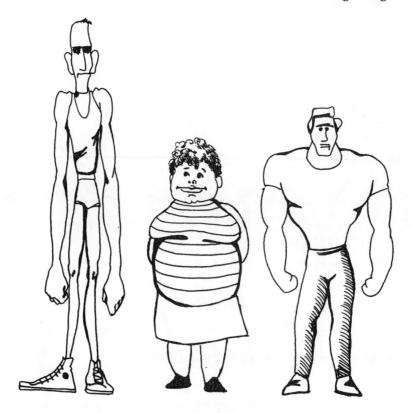

We are all so different!

similar drugs, including tranquilizers, are often electrically
neutral or switched (reversed) in this circuit. If the person needs
to chew or bite into three RNA tablets, for example, before
changing to a normal polarity, then I suggest that he use that
amount at least twice a day. He may need less in a few days and it is
wise for him not to take any on the morning that he is due to be
checked again.

When testing RNA or other glandular products, simply keep
them in your mouth after you bite into them. When you have the
right amount to correct the abnormal switch or neutral circuit,
reverify or double check the muscle testing to make certain that
you can reproduce your results after swallowing the tablets.

Occasionally, especially on a person taking drugs, after you swallow the RNA, recheck the circuit again and you will find that it is abnormal, suggesting that one more RNA tablet is required. It may show this phenomenon rarely because the electrical energy from the RNA tablets are closer to your master computer, the brain, when you have them in your mouth and after you swallow them, additional support is required. Occasionally, a person who is electrically switched will not be corrected by an RNA tablet, but change from a switched state to a neutral state and then require additional RNA to complete the correction to a normal state.

The #1 or master switch circuit may be corrected by other methods in addition to RNA, including yogi, meditation and occasionally a change in the direction he is facing (vivaxis phenomenon). A normal #1 circuit, however, will remain strong

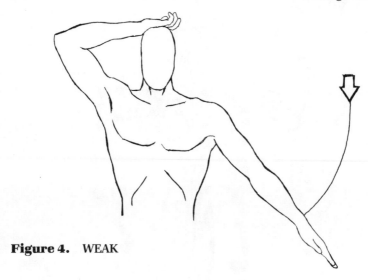

Figure 4. WEAK

in all directions. The last mistake that I see beginners make in performing this test is to place the right hand, in testing, too far back on the head. There are some electrical differences between the front of the head and the back of the head and it is best to place the hand, in testing, on the crown or the top of the head or slightly anterior to the top of the head.

Why does RNA work? Nobody knows for sure. Apparently it stabilizes the electrical discharges in the brain and promotes a more appropriate balance electrically and subsequently, magnetically. There is no doubt that it will change the wrong magnetic poles and correct them within seconds. RNA also improves the ability to concentrate, to remember and sometimes improves balance. Large doses are sometimes necessary. In theory, an individual walking around with his poles upside down is allowing himself to be miocrostressed or shocked every time he steps down on the earth. As previously mentioned, chronically switched patients are seen with long-standing illness, whether physical or emotional, and are often but not always, toxic and allergic individuals. That doesn't mean that simply restoring their electrical flow or polarity will reverse these conditions, but, in theory, the reversal back to normal allows two things to occur.

Number one, only in the individual with proper polarity can we go ahead and get accurate information with the rest of our tests. Thus, it allows us to proceed with the electromagnetic map. Number two, it promotes a positive healing energy. An electrically switched individual often reacts the opposite to vitamins or other things provided for him for healing purposes, no matter how natural and safe they otherwise may be. Coincidentally, the mental and intellectual capacities are sometimes improved by the use of RNA and thus it may have direct therapeutic assistance as well.

In many individuals, however, when taking the proper dose of RNA, experience only a hard-to-describe sense of improvement and mental clarity. Why can't you get the RNA from meat or other beef sources? The RNA tablets are especially processed so that they are never heated, but rather sterilized in a special way that would not destroy the critical protein sequences that make up the product. Heating obviously destroys these sequences and renders cooked products, even though they contain RNA, ineffective for these purposes. The same philosophy holds true for most of the glandular products that I mention later, and I do re-emphasize this philosophy at a later time as well.

Apparently the electroharmonics or frequency admitted by the RNA helps to "unjam the computer". Many of the products, including vitamins and herbs have their own unique electro-frequency, much like a radio signal, which can be picked up via the nervous system by the complex brain computer instantly. That is the most astounding and wonderful part of listening to the wisdom of the body.

At first it was easy for me to shrug that philosophy off as impossible and unscientific, but after having observed the computer capability through many years of testing and then verifying it medically in a scientific way, I have come to respect that this is a new break-through in learning. We will have to wait for the basic scientists and physicists to "catch up" and attempt to verify this mathematically and by appropriate instrumentation. Sometime Bee pollen and spirulina or Brain tissue (Nutritional type) will correct this circuit. These substances all contain RNA.

TEST #2. BRAIN ACTIVITY

Next, we would like to see which side of the brain is working the hardest. With your left arm out and elbow straight, test it to see how strong it is. Now, take your right hand and place it close to your right ear (but don't let it touch) and test the left arm again. Now, let your right hand come around to be close to your left ear and test the left arm again.

INTERPRETATION: The right brain hemisphere is overworking in comparison to its other side when the left arm gets weak. You place your right palm close to the right ear on the same side as the brain overdominance. If your left brain is overworking, you will find, for example, that when you place your right hand close to your left ear with the palm facing the ear, that your left arm will get weak. Refer to the illustrations if you are confused. About seventy-five percent of the patients who come into my office are left hemisphere dominant. They tend to logical, deductive and relatively non-creative and unimaginative people that make good scientists, businessmen, accountants and mathematicians. They make lousy artists, musicians and decorators. If your left brain is usually overworking, most people under stress will either try to logically deal with the stress or blow up. Mr. Spock (on star trek) was a super left-brained person.

If your right ear brain is overworking (your right palm is near your right ear when the muscle gets weak) it indicates a creative, artistic, emotional, usually nonlogical person. Under stress such a person will withdraw, become more childish at times and has a greater chance for detachment from reality and, in extreme cases, develop schizophrenia. Usually such people wait until the stress blows over and deny its existence. The super left-brain person can lead one to extreme perfectionism and obsessive compulsion. He gets into a problem because he cannot accept the fact that life is not as perfect as he expects. One cannot "cure" these character traits with a pill. Twenty percent of my patients are right brain dominant. Ten percent are strong when the palm is placed close to either ear and are said to be hemispherically balanced. It is obvious that most left brained people utilize the right brain at times. I am not certain if there is anyone who only uses one side of his brain at all times. Actually, both sides of the brain are being actively used in the conscious state, so we are referring to the relative dominance.

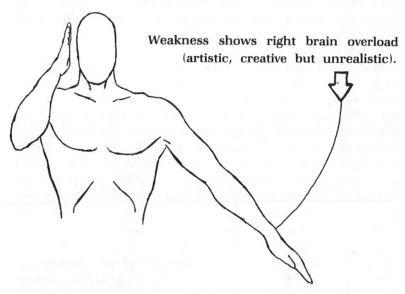

Weakness shows right brain overload (artistic, creative but unrealistic).

Figure 5. TEST # 2 BRAIN ACTIVITY

To help an overly left brain person, learning methods to create, imagine, fantasize and dream are useful! Don't analyze flowers—smell them—enjoy them. When you walk or jog—look around—what smells, sounds and sights are pleasing? Do you simply exercise to practice an obsessive ritual? Take time each day to rest your left brain. To do this, sit comfortably, place your tongue on the ridge behind your front middle upper teeth. Breathe in slowly and deeply. Relax your body and close your eyes and shut out the visual stimuli. Next, picture the first vowel that comes into your mind—a, e, i, o, or u. This will help you to quiet your left brain. If a thought wanders into your brain, think of a vowel and it will eliminate the thought. You are trying to create stillness, giving your left brain a rest and allowing your healing right brain to rejuvenate. Refer to the book in the appendix on Centering, and it will instruct you on more advanced methods of relaxation and right brain activity.

Right brain dominant people can benefit from being more in touch with reality. Reality therapy can be very useful. Logic games and mathematics can be helpful to wake up their left brain function. In general, however, the special exercise of stillness will help balance both sides. Meditators often have balanced hemispheres.

Right sided brain people tend to need potassium and calcium when under stress. They tend to feel comfortable with smaller, more frequent meals. They are of an "acid " nature and do less well with acid foods such as excess meat, sugar, white flour, citrus and tomato. They may have a tendency to an acid taste in the mouth, get mouth ulcers easily, are harder to respond to therapy (especially if their eyes are grey), have an acid type iris pattern, are often wiry, nervous and can be dreamy, spaced-out types. Left brain people tend to have greater need for magnesium

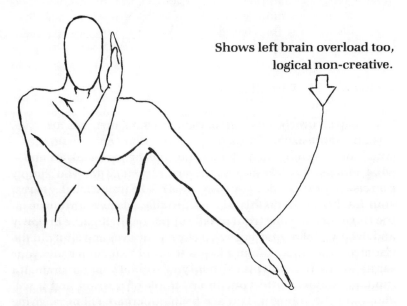

Shows left brain overload too, logical non-creative.

Figure 6.   MUSCLE WEAKNESS

and calcium when under stress, are more alkaline in general, are more sluggish and have more respiratory and food allergies. They often absorb calcium tablets poorly and have a tendency toward tiredness, low blood sugar and fat deposits, especially below the waist. Both types have headache and arthritic tendencies.

A third pattern is the patient who switches from one hemisphere dominance to another during different visits and is usually unstable emotionally and/or physically. He has a higher need for magnesium. Determining exactly whether there is more magnesium need than calcium need at any given point can be done with muscle testing by using the specific points that we will mention later. It should be noted that in some patients after you correct the dominant brain with a mineral or a mental exercise that the opposite side of the brain may show dominance. In other words, if you have a left sided dominance demonstrated by your initial test, and have the patient sing a song or do some other creative right brain activity, it will usually instantly strengthen the left brain dominance. However, when you use minerals, if the patient has a need for calcium and potassium for example, if you give the calcium and it corrects the left brain dominance, then you should check the right brain again, and if it is strong, leave well enough alone. But, if it is weak, see if it is corrected by placing potassium tablets in the mouth of the patient. Remember, you can place the tablets in the mouth and just keep them there because the computer instantly records the frequency from the tablet and will correct the circuits within seconds, indicating you are on the right track. Why should we be concerned with correcting the brain hemisphere dominance? Because it helps to establish a form of normalcy. It creates a goal for better living. Probably one scientist in a hundred has balanced hemispheres or freely moves from the left to the right hemisphere rapidly and comfortably. This is the ideal. That one scientist wll be the one who comes up with original ideas, novel creations and helps mankind to progress. It is extremely uncommon, in theory, for the left brain dominant scientist to move into a new area of creativity in his field, except through a process of logic and deductive reasoning. On the other hand, the left brain scientist is extremely capable of improving on methods based on the ideas of others. He is meticulous, detailed, and is not as likely to be as disillusioned as the right brain dominant individual.

"Retuning" the brain allows a more productive, creative thought process as well as helps retune the nervous system. Right brain dominant individuals are generally having an overactive sympathethic nervous system. Left brain dominant individuals are generally having too much parasympathetic nervous system activity. Obviously, a balance between the hemipsheres and the autonomic nervous system should be one of our goals. Minerals assist in the balance indirectly through providing certain assistance to the creation of the hormones involved with the nervous system. One should not get a sense of false security, however, that they serve as the only necessary therapy in this regard, because more importantly, are methods that allow you to perceive the stress primarily causing your excessive right brain or left brain activity. Techniques in various psychologic schools allow you to feel more comfortable with yourself as well as provide activities to help to reorganize your thinking process and subsequently your hemisphere balance and glandular and nervous system. Many doctors don't wish to emphasize these important corrective psychologic areas, but in cases of extreme right brain or left brain function where "pain" in your life has been created, it is necessary to get to the root of the matter. Cogitative and reality therapy, EST, behavioral modification and biofeedback, and numerous other neopsychologic techniques are beneficial in this regard, depending on the operator and your feeling about the operator or group that you belong to. Deeper in this book are other methods described to help you to help yourself.

Let's go back to analyzing the face. Are there puffy bags under the eyes? In children this usually tips you off to food allergies, especially milk, chocolate and cola problems. In adults, it may indicate the same thing and any food may be the cause at any ages. Often these bags are associated with not sleeping well, depression, hangovers and kidney disturbances. The kidney should always be checked in such patients by energy (muscle) tesing. By muscle testing, many times you are picking up problems that cannot be verified by regular urine and blood tests.

If the kidney reflex is positive, giving natural herbs or support will help that group of people clinically and improve the "bags".

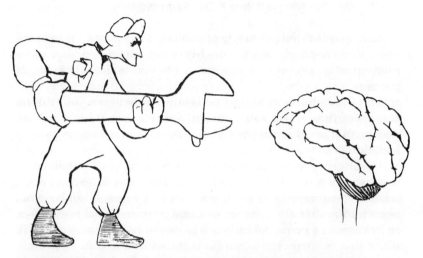

We will talk about other tips for the "kidney people" later.

Swelling between the eyebrows is seen in some cases of liver problems—often the liver or kidney is overloaded with our "good" American diet and showing disturbed magnetic changes.

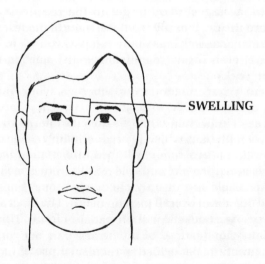

SWELLING

Figure 7. SWELLING

Test # 3: HAIR:

Hair is composed primarily of protein. Because hair is protein, one can do a simple test to roughly determine if you need more high quality protein or amino acids-the building blocks of protein.

With the right hand, simply rub your hair between your thumb and index finger. Use your left arm again to test. (I hope you are resting that arm between tests because it is not necessary to keep it sticking out).

If your arm tests weak while you are rubbing a lock of hair (your means your subject or yourself if someone else is testing you—I tried various devices to see if you can test yourself but have not been happy that any of these are really reproduceably effective) then suspect a protein deficiency of one or more amino acids. To see if this is correct, place a predigested amino acid or protein tablet or powder in your mouth and repeat the test. The test will now be strong if amino acids were low. Remember, every substance has its own wavelength pattern and the brain is giving us answers, because it has the computer cpability to interpret the wavelengths. At the same time, it knows what is ideal for you (not compared to "averages" of other people like blood test answers). If you remove the protein pill from the mouth, the test will again be wrong. You can check it as many times as you wish. It is a real phenomenon, even if our scientists are just starting to understand why it works.

As you rub your fingers over the hair, your fingers are emanating a certain electromagnetic frequency, probably as distinct for each individual as are his fingerprints. As your fingers are in contact with hair, which is predominately made of protein and its derivatives, this reflex will feed information back to the brain. Since your protein consists of different specific amino acids, it is possible to not only check each one, but to subsequently find out about overall protein needs. The exact amount of the exact type of amino acid will correct the circuit. This takes an inappropriately long period of time and we do not currently do this in our practice. We determine the total protein needs as a powder or capsule instead of each amino acid per se. In correlating this with blood testing, it would be wise to remember that the serum protein electrophoresis is a more accurate test than the ordinary albumin and globulin study as found on computers. Often times in protein deficiency states, we find that the albumin is between 3 and 3.5 and these individuals would have been considered marginally low in protein anyway, even by conventional standards. Sometimes we find them below 3, which by World Health Organization criteria indicates low protein. Albumin is made by the liver and it can be influenced by factors other than the amount of protein in your diet. If, however, protein corrects your hair circuit instantly, it would suggest that you would benefit from more protein than you are taking. Those individuals taking very little protein in the diet, especially for many generations, tend to adjust their needs to some extent, even to the point of absorbing it more efficiently through the intestinal tract.

In general, however, our needs should be in the range of .75 to 1 gram per kilogram per day. We are a country of extremes, with one group of individuals probably under consuming protein and another group of individuals gluttonously over consuming it. Vegetarians using appropriate mixtures can safely exist on vegetable protein alone. Milk and eggs and fish are often added to the program to insure additional safety in this regard. Spirulina has been a recent addition that can be enjoyed by vegetarians and meat eaters alike. It is an exceptionally high source of protein and is originally a blue-green algae. An additional bonus to the vegetarian is that it serves as a high source of vitamin B-12.

When I see an abnormal protein reflex in a patient, I feel it is important to find out why it is there. Is the patient improperly following a restricted diet or an unscientific vegetarian diet or reducing diet, all of which are fraught to deliver an improper balance of amino acids. Low stomach acid can sometimes compound the problem and digestive disturbances should be looked into. Sometimes diarrhea, due to pancreas failure or disease of the small or large bowel, will be responsible. Any chronic infection, such as arthritis, liver disease, kidney disease, can produce protein imbalances that would show up in this particular test. Remember that low protein is not always due to a lack of it in the diet. It may be lost in abnormal amounts through the kidney or the bowel. This loss would have to be checked by testing the urine or stool in these special cases. For the most part, however, I find that it is of a dietary nature. Under more stress, we produce more cortisone, which works to the detriment of our protein metabolism. Thus our needs for protein will increase under stressful conditions. Especially extremely stressful conditions such as burns, trauma, and after surgery. What does chronic stress do for protein needs? At least a certain portion of our chronically stressed patients indicate to us that essential amino acids, either in a predigested or a separated form, are useful. Dr. Philpot in Oklahoma City suggests that in some of the extremely complicated allergic states to chemicals and foods, certain problems with vitamins and amino acids are also important. In such states specific amino acids, such as cysteine, or ornothine or glycine are useful. Amino acids create our immunity or defense system. If protein is deficient you have a higher tendency to have an abnormal expression of the delayed immunity system, which is responsible for helping us fight cancer and certain bacterial and viral illnesses. Thus, the hair relfex has a lot of implications and can guide us as to whether a serum albumin is truly correlating with an ideal of acceptable state to the brain computer. This may be better than using blood tests in comparing us with other "average" people, some of which may also have defective hair tests. The hair relfex does not correlate with mineral imbalances in the hair. It should be noted that the hair test can be abnormal in individuals very sensitive to petroleum compounds, if they have sprayed the hair with such compounds. If you have dyed hair, it is better to probably work with the roots, as you may get a false weakness if your body is expressing its desire to be intolerant to the dye. I have found that most dyed hair, however, does not give an abnormal test unless there is a need for protein in addition. Blood tests may pick up other types of protein abnormalities not seen with the hair test, so both of these are useful.

The Nobel Prize in physics for 1980 was awarded in the area of the unified field theory of elemental particles and forces. This was proposed by Maxwell a hundred years ago and popularized by Einstein. This book is not the appropriate place to discuss metaphysics, quantum theory and advanced neurophysiology, but that is where our correlations will be found.

We, as healers, should stand in awe of God's greatest creation-man himself and that which separates him from other primates—his brain. Will we ever unravel all its mysteries? Not if we look at brain research in a mechanistic, reductionistic way.

TEST # 4: LOWER BRAIN OR HYPOTHALAMUS:

With your right hand, touch the finger pads of your big and little finger together and keep them that way for this test (we will call this our *loop*). It is a mini-electrical circuit (Fig. 8). With the pad of your middle finger as your "toucher", touch the spot on your forehead just between your eyebrows. If your left arm goes weak at that time, then you have a bad regulating circuit in the lower brain area. It may be corrected by RNA in some cases or hypothalamus supplement found with nutritional doctors and

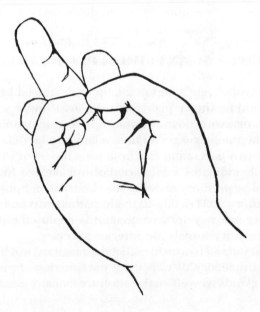

Figure 8. AUGMENTATION LOOP

some health stores* or by meditation, prayer or deep relaxation methods. One of these procedures may keep it balanced better than others. This lower brain circuit roughly correlates with the hypothalamus and is an important test circuit. This area is where your gland control and your autonomic nervous system begin. Your appetite, water needs, sleep areas and many other important basic functions are found here. This area is often chemically wrong in chronic depression or major stressful overloading of any type. A chronic bad circuit suggests that your glands and nervous system are not working together. Hypoglycemia, depression, appetite, thirst, weight and energy problems are frequent. In the female patient the periods become irregular even with normal pelvic exams.

Treat the basic stress overload, support the brain hemispheres and support the hypothalamic area with hypothalamus extract (a food extract-not a drug). Some vegetarians would prefer the RNA in Bee Pollen, propolis or spirulina to see if they will correct this circuit. Don't use the product if it fails to correct the circuit.

TEST # 5: ANTERIOR PITUITARY:

Again keep your right hand in a loop as described before and make your middle finger pad touch the area under your nose (halfway between your nose and your lip). If your strong left arm goes weak, then it suggests you have a bad pituitary circuit. The pituitary has two parts, and this area tests the front or anterior part. It usually indicates a decreased or imbalanced function. It can be helped by pituitary extract (a food extract) or homeopathic anterior pituitary. NOTE: If both the hypothalamus and pituitary gland circuits are wrong, hypothalamus replacement usually corrects both, as it controls the anterior pituitary.

The pituitary gland has been called the master gland because it provides hormone signals to control the function of the thyroid and adrenal glands as well as the sex hormones. A pituitary that

*Refer to appendix for manufacturers of glandulars (proto-morphogens).

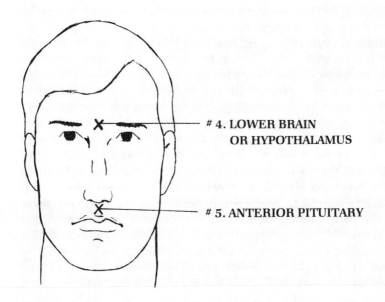

Figure 9.

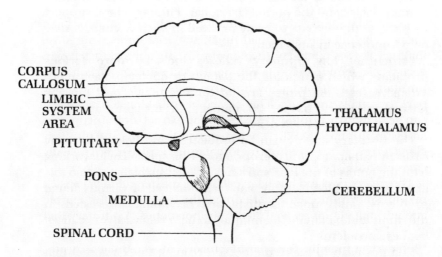

Figure 10.

does not match its ideal output or capability can be picked up by the reflex just described. Remember, we are measuring biologic energies usually indicating less than ideal function. We assume that the special part of your brain that is interpreting these reflexes *knows what is right for you.* Sometimes the over-functioning of a gland will not be found by this method of testing—such as overmaking growth hormone causing acro-megaly or gigantism or overmaking a hormone (prolactin) that causes women to secrete milk abnormally and have a loss of periods. In other words, some pituitary conditions may occur which will not give a positive test by this method and a glandular specialist (endocrinologist) may be helpful in these cases.

Usually a mild to moderate deficiency of the pituitary gland *relative to the patient's ideal*, not necessarily shown on blood studies or X-rays, will be picked up by this reflex. The patient with a chronic mild low-output pituitary, which may be related to tissue changes in the skull area that houses the gland or hereditary factors, will often feel improved with pituitary. This type of patient will be short in stature, small graceful hands, intelligent, and quick thinking usually, fine hair, pale complexion and often have a dental overbite or temporomandibular syndrome (to be talked about later). Breast development is small in many cases and the periods irregular. Pituitary gland support may cause the breasts to grow or swell in such women. It may help impotence in such men.

Sometimes low pituitary reflexes indicate more serious problems which can guide the patient or doctor to seek more extensive tests. Examples are (a) tumors that crowd out the normal pituitary tissue, (b) damage to the pituitary from accidents or a hard birth delivery.

The pituitary energy can be influenced and helped in many cases by osteopaths and chiropractors who specialize in working with the bones of the face and skull (cranial specialists). Also this gland, with its blood supply, can be influenced by various dental problems, and more dentists are becoming interested in nutrition and balancing techniques to help relieve stress caused by these problems.

I do not wish to make the person reading this book feel that muscle testing is a specific tool that eliminates the need for common sense and continued cooperation with his physician. It provides a tool to pick up subtle differences as compared to *your ideal* and is useful in providing a clue in early conditions even beyond the hair or blood tests. It is more useful in underactive than overactive conditions. More complex methods of muscle testing, however, can determine answers more specifically and discriminate between underactive and overactive states.

Review So Far:

1. Muscle energy testing is a useful general guide to disturbances in the system.
2. It is not specific and should be interpreted realizing its limitations.
3. In milder problems, it provides a guide for self-help using natural therapy methods.
4. In more severe cases, a holistic physician is recommended to work with you.

STEPS TO FOLLOW SO FAR:

TEST # 1. Are you switched, thus giving the tester inaccurate answers? To correct, take RNA.

TEST # 2. Consider which side of the brain is over-working—write it down—check it again later.

TEST # 3. Hair. Do you need more high quality protein?

TEST # 4. Is your hair a major stress receiving center—the deeper brain circuits and hypothalamus, not up to par? Consider relaxing or de-stressing methods to help first and use hypothalamus glandular extracts.

TEST # 5. Is the pituitary balanced? If not, check circuit #4 and fix it first. If it does not automatically fix this circuit as well, then analyze the following:

If no major unexplained weight change or visual or neurologic change has occured, take pituitary glandular or see a holistic practitioner to see if a dental or cranial problem is contributing. If problems persist, he will get further tests. The posterior pituitary is not measured by this reflex, and we will not deal with this area.

TEST # 6. UPPER CRANIAL JAMMING TEST

At the very top of the skull the loop test should be done with the pad of the middle right finger. If the left arm loses power, then some type of jamming of the skull bones is present. Just like stubbing your finger, the skull bones can be jarred or impacted so that problems usually missed by brain scans or X-rays persist for years. Some conditions that can be helped by fixing the jam include relief of dizzy spells, relief of headaches, mental sluggishness, some learning disorders and many other remote problems. Note that there are many causes for these complaints and skull jamming is only one of them. Birth injuries, old falls and auto accidents are the three most common causes of jamming that I see, but dental problems can cause it as well.

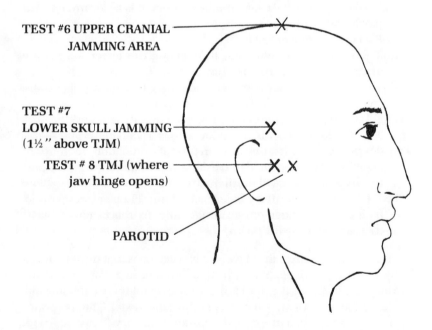

Figure 11.   Test 6.

TEST #7. LOWER SKULL JAMMING TEST

Test just in front of the tip of the ear (see illustration), using the loop technique with the right middle finger pad. After touching this area in front of the tip of the right ear, bring your right hand over to touch the same spot in front of the tip of your left ear. If the left arm gets weak when closing the reflex, it indicates a jamming of some of the lower skull bones and should be investigated by an osteopath or a chiropractor knowledgeable in cranial treatments. In many of these cases injuries and dental problems cause the problem and can result in headaches, jaw pain, neck pain, dizziness or hearing disturbances. There are some skull jamming problems that these tests can not detect.

One can learn so much from the face, so don't give up—you are learning a magnetic map that can help you and your family.

TEST #8. FEEL THE JOINT (TMJ)

Place the two finger pads (right index and middle finger) over this joint just in front of the ear on both sides and see if it causes weakness in the left arm.

The TMJ joint is important and a major disturbance should be corrected by better nutrition and a dentist who is trained to measure and balance the joint. Sometimes skull jamming causes the problem and the doctor that corrects cranial problem is again the best for this problem. As these doctors and dentists understand each other's problems, let them decide which is more important.

Other causes of TMJ problems include muscle spasm due to emotional problems, causing one to excessively set or clench his jaw or grind his teeth. Biofeedback and emotional treatment can help in these cases. Lastly, we find arthritis, both osteo and rheumatoid types, in this joint and they may be more difficult to treat. Special X-rays are usually necessary to verify this problem, including close-up views with the mouth open and closed.

Perhaps you have other clues that you have a jaw imbalance. Sometime patients with TMJ problems have pain in the jaw joint. If you have had trouble finding your jaw joint, just open and close your mouth while you keep your two fingers just in front of your ear and you will feel the exact area where the jaw moves as it fits into the skull bone. That is the TMJ joint. Sometimes as you touch it, you will feel a pop or a click. Other times you can hear the click. This is the sign of a disturbance in the joint, even if there is no pain. Another way to check for disturbance in this area is to look in the mirror as you open your mouth. Does your mouth open smoothly, evenly and straight down? If it zigzags or makes an S, veering to one side or another at the completion of the opening, it indicates spasm in some of the muscles on one side or another, usually the side that it draws toward. This is another sign of jaw joint imbalance. Dentists grade the jaw joint problem in various ways, and in milder cases the teeth can be rebalanced or the muscles inside the mouth and jaw can be stretched by acu-pressure-type techniques, which is called a Nimmo technique. In more severe stages of dislocation of the jaw joint or extensive arthritis problems, surgery may be necessary, however. The longer you wait, the more problems are apt to occur. Many cases of recurrent neck pain and upper shoulder pain, as well as re-current headaches, are caused by jaw imbalance. In the cases where the first bone under the skull, called the atlas, seems to twist out of place, it is related to improper jaw balance. A band at the top of the head is usually related to improper jaw balance. This is because the fascia and tissues that connect at the jaw, go to many different parts of the head and neck area. They can sometimes influence ringing in the ears and hearing problems because they are internally related to the tube that runs from the ear to the throat, which is called the Eustachian tube. Many people have an imbalance of their jaw, which pops and grinds and clicks and hurts, with very little problem otherwise. The patient that is more likely to get neck pain or headache pain is the one who is either toxic or has old injury patterns, so that the jaw imbalance causing a tissue pull complicates matters with an old jamming from a head injury or tailbone injury or neck injury, especially after old whiplashes. If the jaw imbalance was not present, possibly the body would be able to adjust to the old injury and "keep the area quiet". Many doctors might disagree on whether the jaw injury or the neck injury is more important, but I think it is necessary to put the controversy of chickens and eggs aside, and to treat the areas that can be treated, and to realize that the fascia and other tissue that connects one part of the body to another does not show up on X-rays and was sincerely taught to every doctor in his first year in medical school, but often ignored after that.

TEST # 9. JAW REFLEX

Without testing anything with your right arm, see if your left arm is strong in the clear (without touching anything with the right hand). This should be done to check for a tired muscle before any test is done so you are making a comparison between before and after test response. Also, it is obvious that the left arm should rest between tests.

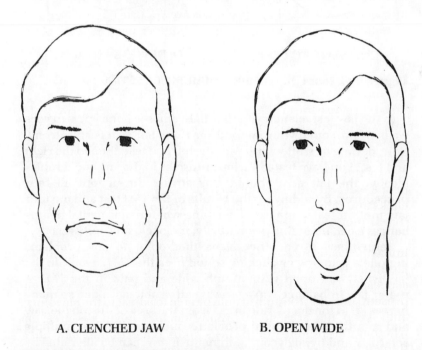

A. CLENCHED JAW   B. OPEN WIDE

Figure # 12.   JAW MUSCLE TESTING

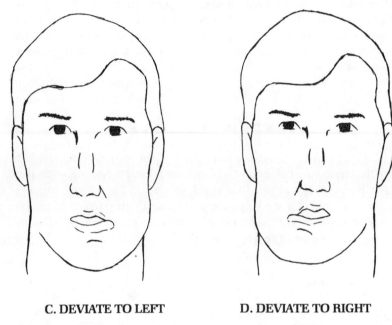

C. DEVIATE TO LEFT   D. DEVIATE TO RIGHT

Figure # 12 (cont'd).   MORE JAW MUSCLE TESTING

In the jaw test, clench your jaw tight and see if the left arm goes weak. If not, open your jaw and see if the left arm is still strong. Now, deviate or shift your jaw to the left and test, then to the right and test. You have tested various muscles in the jaw and temples ideally, the left arm should stay strong throughout all four procedures. By adding up the results of the TMJ test and the four jaw motion tests, one can determine when major dental disturbances exist, including prematurity, malocclusion and overbite.

Remember, three other signs that point to jaw problems include a grinding or clicking sound over the TMJ, a shift in the jaw when you open your mouth wide and pain in the TMJ. A major jaw imbalance can aggravate all problems, since so many nerves go to the deep brain areas from the area of the tongue, jaw and mouth. Even general problems such as allergies, multiple sclerosis and hypoglycemia, to name a few, can be alleviated by helping the jaw areas.

TEST # 10. PAROTID

One inch in front of the jaw joint on both sides, is a point that relates to one of the major glands that provides saliva. Saliva helps first break down starches, but Dr. Goodhart feels that good saliva flow is helpful in allowing the brain to better identify the food you are chewing and signals the body to provide better digestion deeper inside. If this reflex causes the left arm to get weak (check both sides), then think of why the saliva is suppressed. Drugs can do it, emotional tension can do it, and rarely a disease known as Sjogren's syndrome, due to destruction of the gland, can do it. This syndrome consists of dry mouth, dry eyes and arthritis or rheumatism. Getting to the cause is our goal, and parotid glandular supplement can help. Chewing food more slowly is helpful. At times patients who don't appear to be "absorbing their supplements" are helped by adding parotid to their program if this reflex is abnormal. Use the loop technique to find this spot.

Now Let's Review:

TEST # 6 on the very top of the skull looks for jamming of the upper skull.*

TEST # 7 just before the tip of the ear check a part of the lower skull area to rule out jamming.

TEST # 8 TMJ area is tested in the area just before the middle of the ear.

TEST # 9 the four steps in looking for jaw and dental problems.

TEST # 10 checks for saliva flow from the parotid gland on both sides.

*Doctors trained in AK (Applied Kinesiology) have a more elaborate way of testing for skull problems and can find problems missed by our screening tests.

TEST # 11. POTASSIUM

Find the angle of the jaw. Now run your finger forward and you will feel a notch. Just above this notch on the flat part of the jaw bone, place the looped middle finger pad and test the left arm. If it is weak on the left side, then potassium is probably low. The blood does not always show this because of chemical shifting. Common reasons for low potassium include water pills, large amounts of licorice, some kidney problems, vomiting and diarrhea and stress with overmaking of cortisone by the body. The potassium point is *only* on the left side. Some right brain over-reactors will need potassium. (See TEST # 2).

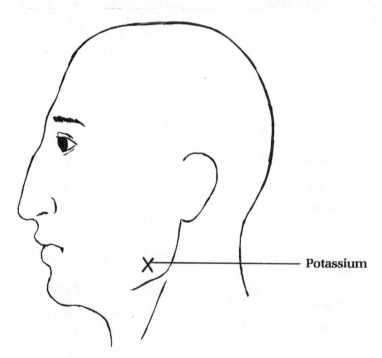

Potassium

Figure # 13. TEST # 11

TEST # 12. SODIUM

On the same location of the right jaw, you will find a point for sodium. A weakened left arm indicates a deficiency of sodium. Sodium, a component of salt, is necessary for life, but too much can promote edema (water retention) and high blood pressure. A deficiency can result in light-headaches, low blood pressure and tiredness. It can result from low adrenal output, vomiting, diarrhea, certain kidney problems, water pills and certain uncommon states such as the ill-feeling after an injury, burn or operation, or after a serious illness. In these latter cases, brain hormones cause an abnormal holding of water, and restriction of water by mouth is the main part of the treatment. An abnormal sodium reflex is not common even when one has a bad adrenal reflex.

TEST # 13. PANCREAS AND SINUS

Draw an imaginary line from the center of the eye downward on the face and another line horizontally from the bottom of the nose. Where these lines meet is a small hole on both sides of the face. Place the thumb of the right hand on the right point and the pad of the right index finger on the left point and test the left arm. If the arm goes weak, the pancreas is possibly not functioning up to par. Is there hypoglycemia? Is there diabetes in the family? The reflex is a guide to ask further questions and put the evidence together. It should be checked with another pancreas test to be discussed later. At times, sinus trouble can allow the same test to be positive, since some of the sinus system is located near this area. This point will be helped by giving chromium in many cases if there is no active sinus trouble. Give some chromium or Brewers yeast and see if it reverses the reflex.

There are other face tests, but enough have been covered to give you a great deal of information. Before we go to the body for more information, let us discuss the eye.

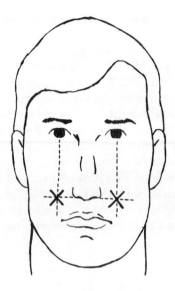

Figure # 14.   TEST # 13 PANCREAS AND/OR SINUS (MAXILLARY)

The eye should be clear and bright. The sclera or white part should not have major blood vessel enlargement or be discolored. A yellowish sclera is seen with liver disease or, rarely, with blood that is breaking down too fast. There are many signs on the outer and inner eye that are too complicated to cover here, but some signs seen in the iris can be reviewed. The eye is an extension of the brain, and like the brain, has a map on the colored part (iris) that can help you see problems both hereditary and acquired. A master iris diagnostician can pick up all kinds of problems by reviewing the sclera, iris and other parts of the eye, but let's cover a few basics.*

The inner one third of the iris corresponds to the intestinal tract. The part closest to the pupil corresponds to the stomach. An underactive stomach (one that produces too little acid) causes the fibers to darken and clump just around the pupil.

*Refer to the appendix if you are interested in learning about this area in more detail.

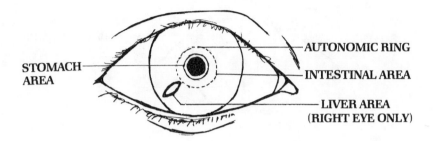

Figure # 15.

The intestinal area (refer to the map in the appendix) is shown by the inner one third and is surrounded by the autonomic wreath or ring. Normally the area within the wreath is the same color or slightly darker than the rest of the iris. With constipation, this area will be darker than usual, and the whole zone will be more dilated or wider than average.

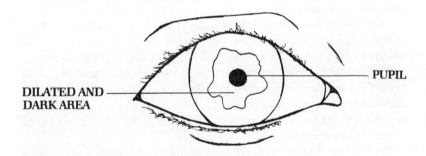

Figure # 16. EYE/BODY CONNECTION

The inner edge of the wreath may show dark areas that suggest accumulated crusts or material in the colon. At times, marked dilations outward of the intestinal area may occur. This usually indicates sacs or diverticula in these areas of the intestine.

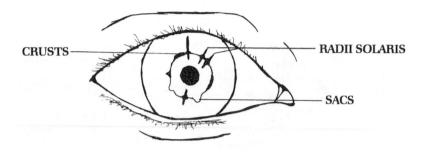

CRUSTS ———— ———— RADII SOLARIS

———— SACS

Figure # 17.

Radii solaris is a sign of bowel toxicity. It also suggests possible hidden parasites in the colon. The dark lines seem to cut into the iris and are best seen by shining a light at an angle on the iris. Normally, a light and a magnifying glass are used to study the iris. All of the organs can be found in the iris, and a system exists by which the non-physician as well as the interested doctor can study this method. Several books discussing the study are reviewed in the appendix.

I discussed a small part of iris diagnosis to let you know a little about this area, but mainly to get you interested in learning more about this subject. It is useful in learning hereditary weaknesses and general problems, but again is not specific and must be correlated with the patient's problems verbally and nonverbally. Muscle tests and eye diagnoses generally correlate well if done accurately. As we will concentrate on muscle tests in this book, we will not proceed with iris diagnosis.

To accurately provide self help or work naturally with friends and family, I suggest that you learn and use eye diagnosis and muscle testing and listen to the problems. Do *not* make a religion out of muscle testing or iris diagnosis. It will be an easy habit to fall into when you become an expert in any of these areas. To rely only on these areas is part of reductionism.

Many other parts of the face can be helpful in diagnosis. Look at the gums. Are they overgrowing? This is caused by drugs at times. Are they black between the teeth? Think of lead poisoning. Are they red and inflammed? Can be caused by infection, nutritional problems or hormone imbalance, especially a lack of sex hormone.

Is there bad breath? This indicates a dental, sinus or intestinal problem in most cases.

Look at the tongue. Is there an irregular white pattern on it? Usually this indicates an allergy. A general white or yellow color is seen with intestinal imbalances.

Is there a regurgitation of acid sour material as seen with hiatus hernia or a weak upper stomach valve?

Is there a bitter taste in the mouth as seen in liver or bile problems?

A metallic taste also usually reflects liver problems, though can be found with incorrect metal in the teeth or body.

Is the face swollen? This is found in thyroid deficiency, heavy drinking, allergies and kidney disease.

Now let's prepare a check-list of the reflexes we have learned so far. Mark the positives down. Later you can double check the reflexes, interpret what they mean (more important than the reflexes themselves) and see if you can reverse any weak reflexes with the proper nutritional factor. Before the review, we need to show you proof that the vitamins and glandulars or herbs discussed really are able to help. They should thus reverse a bad reflex in seconds.

Everything on the face of the earth of natural and synthetic origin has its own special wavelength due to its unique molecular structure. The computer in your brain can identify whether this wavelength is agreeable or not. One man's meat is another man's poison, so that what is okay for one person may be against the next.

Since we have a magnetic energy and complex wavelength surrounding us, when we place a substance within a half inch from our bodies (whether in our mouths or in our hand) a complicated interaction of energies occurs and the brain records these relationships. If the energy is incorrect, it will cause a mini shock to the computer like TEST # 1, and the brain shows its disturbance by weakening all the muscles of the body. Since we are testing one of them, it should stay strong with a good message and get weak with a bad one.

GOOD	BAD	SUPPLEMENT
1. Switch #1		RNA
2. Right/Left		Minerals
3. Protein		Protein
4. Hypothalamus		Hypothalamus
5. Pituitary		or Pituitary
6. Upper Cranial Jam		Help from a holistic practitioner.
7. Lower Cranial Jam		
8. TMJ		Help from a holistic practitioner.
9. Jaw Muscles		

    a. clench
    b. open
    c. deviate left
    d. deviate right

10. Saliva		Parotid
11. Potassium		Potassium
12. Sodium		Sodium
13. Pancreas (Sinus)		Pancreas

Face-color
    Swollen—generally
        under eyes
Breath
Gums—color, growth
Tongue—color
Teeth—cavities, disease-
        crooked
Eyes—sclera, iris, pupil

Section V

THROAT AND CHEST

 he two main reflexes in the throat are lymph nodes and thyroid.

TEST # 14: LYMPH NODES

Make a loop and with pad of the middle right finger touch the area in the soft part of the neck, just under the angle of the jaw. Test both sides and write it down. The magnetic flow on one side of the body is the opposite polarity of the other, so lymph channel testing may be positive only on one side. Test the left arm again. If weak, consider methods to clear the lymph nodes which are backing up with lymph toxins. The lymph is a special fluid that carries waste away from all cells through special channels. This fluid is filtered though the lymph nodes. This reflex is positive even before the nodes get large. Larger nodes are usually seen in children. They sometimes get large for more serious reasons.

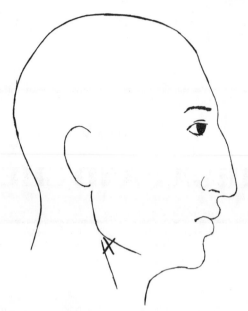

Figure # 18.   TEST # 14 LYMPH NODES

The reflexes for lymph problems in these areas may indicate a general low grade toxicty of the lymph or be limited to this area which drains the area of the tonsil. If tonsils have been removed, it still can indicate a local problem. The area in the old tonsil bed and the area behind the tonsil may be a source of pus.

Lymph problems in patients sometimes cause lymph node soreness or enlargement, a positive spleen reflex, or rarely, spleen enlargement and the lymphatic rosary or spots in the iris of the eye. They appear best in lighter irises and look like small white balls around the outer edge of the iris. There may be only a few. In most adults we find lymph reflex problems not associated with actual enlargement of the lymph glands and certainly we are not looking at all the lymph glands when we merely touch the reflexes under the angle of the jaw. If you wish to explore the other lymph nodes that often are enlarged, they should be both felt for as well as tested by making the loop and check under the armpits and the groins, over the collar bones and along the front and back muscles of the neck. Helping the lymph reflex, which indirectly indicates an overload of the lymph system, in theory, can be done in many ways. There are certain glandular support products which contain lymph tissues, thymus and spleen or parotid tissue. Herb formulas and vitamin A are useful in these patients in most cases. Homeopathic drops from various companies are now being prepared that would reverse the reflexes in seconds. Probably the most in-depth way of helping besides the method just discussed includes exercise, because the lymph system works better with more activity, with deeper breathing and with proper eliminations. Many individuals use a mini trampoline, which comes commercially under a variety of names, and bounce on it for ten to fifteen minutes a day. This is one of the most effective ways to promote lymph flow and is easier on the knees, back and ankles than jogging. Rapid walking and jogging, however, are effective ways to "clear these channels". Manipulation and acupuncture can also be useful if done correctly. Special manipulation efforts directed toward the first rib area is helpful because the main channels where the lymph ducts connect to the blood system are reflexly connected near the first rib. The first rib on the left side connects with the main duct that drains the body and the right first rib connects with the drainage areas from a portion of the lung, heart and head areas. Massage and manipulation of these areas can be carried out by a variety of professionals, but usually is done by chiropractors or osteopaths.

LYMPH
ACCUMULATIONS

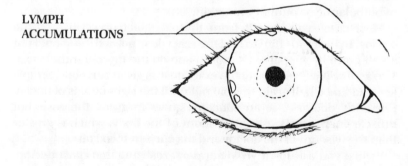

Figure # 19.

TEST # 15 : THYROID

Place the right hand palm over the front of the neck. The thyroid gland lies under the hand. If the left arm goes weak on testing, there is something wrong with the thyroid.

The thyroid is an important gland that helps maintain energy. Some patients who are overweight will be helped by giving thyroid. Most patients with a positive reflex are low in their thyroid output as compared to their ideal. The thyroid blood test (T-7) is more accurate in finding an overactive thyroid than one with underactive function.

Patients with overactive thyroid glands (hyperthyroidism) have (a) a fine tremor or shakiness of the tongue and hands, (b) weight loss, (c) warmth bothers them more than cold, (d) inner tension or anxiety, (e) an enlarged gland or sometimes a local area of growth in the area of enlarged gland, (f) menstrual irregularities, (g) heart palpitations, (h) fatigue.

Patients with this problem should consult their physician because "living with it" can result in serious problems.

Patients with low thyroid function (hypothyroidism) usually have (a) tiredness, (b) apathy, (c) dry skin, (d) dry hair, (e) weight gain, or inability to lose weight, (f) sometimes an enlarged gland, (g) occasionally a hearing decrease, (h) constipation, and (i) a temperature below 97.6° under the armpit.

The thyroid may rarely be low not because the gland is sick, but because of low iodine in the body, drugs that block the gland, or low hypothalamic or pituitary function.

Most cases will benefit from thyroid tablet prescribed by the doctor. In order for him to find the exact dose needed, he should put a half grain in the patient's mouth and do the thyroid muscle test. The arm will be weak until the exact dose is given correctly. Simply keep adding a half grain thyroid pill until the right dose is obtained. Currently doctors use an educated guess in giving the dose, but muscle energy tests use the wisdom of the body, which is greater than the wisdom of the doctor and the current blood test.

Before you ask for thyroid support, realizing that most doctors will not give it to you if the blood test is "normal", check the following relfexes and if they are abnormal, correct them.

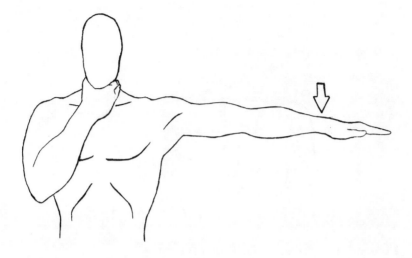

Figure # 20.   TEST # 15 THYROID

(a) Hypothalamus—give hypothalamus gland support—a food extract.

(b) Pituitary—corrects with pituitary gland support—a food extract.

(c) Iodine reflex (to be described next)—give iodine or kelp.

Now, after you correct these circuits, recheck the thyroid reflex. If it is still abnormal, you will need a thyroid hormone. If you have a problem finding a cooperating physician, write to one of the groups listed in the appendix. Remember, a chiropractor is legally prohibited from dispensing drugs, including thyroid, but can use a nondrug thyroid extract which is sometimes helpful.

TEST # 16: IODINE CIRCUIT

Find the soft part on the top of your breast bone (sternum). Now, slide the fingers down the breast bone about 1 to 2 inches. You should feel a slight elevation of bone in most cases, just lateral to this area is the front of the second rib. In the soft area between the

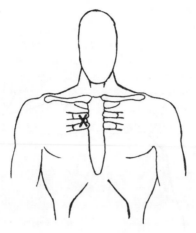

Figure # 21.   TEST # 16 IODINE CIRCUIT

second and third rib, just next to the breast bone is the iodine point. It is only on the right side. With the looped hand, touch the spot with the right middle finger. Test the left arm.

Correct any weakness with kelp or organic iodine. Too much iodine can cause thyroid problems in a few people. Only a little is needed. Rarely, iodine causes enlarged parotid glands, metal taste in mouth or skin rash.

TEST # 17: VITAMIN C

It is possible to evaluate your need for various vitamins and minerals. In the past, doctors and nutritionists guessed about your needs and compared what you were eating with the RDA established by the government. The RDA determines nutrient doses in the average population that prevents gross nutritional disease.

These guidelines have their place, and I am sure the government is doing the best it can based on current experimental information. Muscle testing, however, can tell you what your needs are compared to the ideal you. These needs are not constant and will vary to some extent day by day. That is one reason I decided to let the public learn the reflexes. The health oriented community can monitor itself against too many vitamins and minerals, and too little.

Vitamin C (ascorbic acid). In the soft area just below the middle of your left collar bone is a Vitamin C point. Touch this spot with the loop technique (right middle finger pad). If the left arm goes weak on testing, then more vitamin C is needed. Let us understand how the body computer records, because we are basically learning computer programing with a more sophisticated computer than ever invented by man.

The methods that we describe to determine the dose of vitamin C tells you your needs and generally applies to other vitamins and minerals as well.

If you show a need for Vitamin C, place a 500 mg. capsule or tablet in your mouth, or better yet, just hold it in your right hand. After all, the wavelength of the vitamin is being computed and the strength of the frequency is related to the dose. If your left arm is judged via a muscle test, keep checking the test arm after placing more and more in the hand. The body will tell you when your exact needs are computed as the left arm then becomes strong. If you place one pill too many in the hand, the arm again gets weak. Thus, the body computes both an underdose and an overdose. This is how the body works if you are currently on no vitamins or only a small "RDA" amount.

The second way that the body records its need is that it records only a small overdose and not an underdose. If you need 1500 mg. of Vitamin C, for example, your body, using the second computing method, would show a strong muscle with one capsule, two capsules, three capsules. The fourth 500 mg. capsule added to the hand would cause weakness (an overdose).

Either of the two methods can lead you to accurate information about herbs, vitamins or minerals. If you are already taking large amounts of Vitamin C, you probably cannot compute accurately and one pill after another will test strong as the body has already received so much it has to adapt to the amount and make new rules.

Thus, there are three ways to read the computer. But, what if the body doesn't like the particular kind of Vitmain C? Holding the entire bottle first can tell you that, especially if it is in a glass bottle. If your arm gets weak when holding a full bottle, then the body is telling you to find another type. The frequency of a substance can pass through unleaded glass. For some natural substances with much energy, such as herbs, an accurate answer can even pass through a plastic bottle.

What could make Vitamin C disagreeable? The base of nearly all Vitamin C is corn. If the person is sensitive to corn, it may cross over to the Vitamin C. Other times it is the citrus added, or rosehips. Pure rosehip capsules are a good alternative to regular Vitamin C.

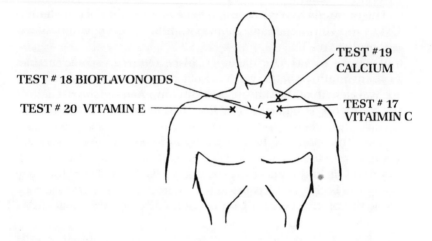

TEST #19
CALCIUM

TEST # 18 BIOFLAVONOIDS

TEST # 20 VITAMIN E

TEST # 17
VITAIMIN C

Figure # 22.

TEST # 18: BIOFLAVONOIDS

Nowhere in nature do we find Vitamin C alone. It is found with a group of other compounds known as bioflavonoids. Rutin and hesperidin are examples. These compounds are useful in improving blood vessel strength. Easy bruising and small blood spots under the skin should be treated with bioflavonoids (a non drug). The point to indicate this vitamin complex is under the left collar bone. Test it with the loop. The precise point is found by touching the top of the breast bone and then sliding your finger toward the left and encountering the collar bone. Feel the collar bone on the top and then on the bottom and the point is found on the left side where the lower part of the collar bone and the breast bone meet. This is the bioflavonoid point. It is in the softness or tissue, just lateral to the sternum or breast bone.

TEST # 19: CALCIUM

Calcium is found in meats, certain sprouts, vegetables, milk, and eggs. In people who do not take dairy products, especially children, supplemental calcium may be useful. Also allergic patients tend to use calcium less well inside the body. A Canadian investigator found that Vitamin D and calcium were very helpful in controlling asthma.

Calcium is more likely to be needed when there is a deficiency in stomach acid production, in the toxic/allergic patient and in the patient with left brain overstimulation (see TEST # 2). Calcium lactate or gluconate may be used or herbs rich in calcium may be helpful.

The calcium point is located just above the left collar bone in the soft area just above the middle of the bone. Vitamin C below, calcium above. Calcium is one of the major elements needed by the body and is primarily stored along with magnesium and phosphorus. The blood requires a steady amount of calcium, so over a long period of time, if there is a deficiency in the diet, it will be reflected in the bone because the stores there will have to give up their calcium gradually and this will cause certain diagnostic problems. It is possible to measure ionizable calcium, but the usual calcium test, run by the doctor, measures primarily the calcium that is bound to protein in the blood. If the protein is low, then the calcium will falsely appear lower than it really is. On the other hand, if the body isn't getting proper calcium from the diet and has to steal it from the bones in an abnormal amount, it will usually not be reflected in the blood tests. Hair calcium values in such cases may be either very high or low, depending on how long the process has been going on. Female hormone is helpful in keeping the calcium in the bone, and a lack of female hormone speeds up the loss of calcium from the bone and promotes a weakening of the bony tissue over a period of time, which makes one more susceptible to broken hips and backs in years ahead. Thus, female hormone, in proper amounts, is a helpful product to use for most menopausal women, providing certain rules are met. These rules are complex and should be followed with your doctor's advice.

Dr. Royal Lee discovered that besides vitamin D, allowing the calcium to better enter the body, that essential unsaturated fatty acids (vitamin F) allowed the calcium to be utilized at the tissue level in a better way. But some individuals, especially those not utilizing cold pressed oil, especially sunflower oil, might have a mild vitamin F deficiency and subsequently show signs of muscular irritability or muscle cramps. I have several patients that note that when they take safflower, sunflower or lecithin, they have fewer cramps in their muscles. What they are expressing is that they have discovered the same thing that Dr. Royal Lee explained, but they don't realize it. So, in looking for the reasons behind muscle cramps, irritability, emotionally and physically—and sometimes muscle soreness—it is wise to check the calcium point, but also the hydrochloric acid point, the magnesium point and the vitamin F point.

You are starting to realize as I review these points that it is not the finding of a problem at the various electrical circuits that is important. It is the interpretation of what it means in relationship to other points. Basic physiology is very helpful in this regard, and thus the reason why something doesn't work is not always because you made an improper evaluation, but because you have a lack of understanding of how it relates to some other point. Nevertheless, there are many lay individuals using this technique already, and a majority of them feel better and are grateful to have a system to allow them to be more precise in their choices. I have seen individuals taking over $100.00 worth of supplements per month unnecessarily, who may just as well be on a few specific things that the body wishes, and accomplish much more good. Of course the reverse is sometimes true and there are individuals that are apparently so run down, in spite of "normal" X-rays and blood tests, that a lot of different nutritional support tools are needed for the first few months. Additional magnetic checks will indicate less and less support is needed as the body gets stronger.

TEST # 20: VITAMIN E

A controversial vitamin which can lose the confusion attached to it by listening to the wisdom of the body instead of scientists who probably have incomplete information on the uses of Vitamin E inside of the body. The same holds true of Vitamin C. The body knows if it needs the vitamin and, if so, what dose is required.

The vitamin E point is located just below the middle of the right collar bone. Since we are using the same method of testing the whole way throughout the book, I will not keep repeating that the right middle finger pad with the thumb and small finger touching "closes the circuit" and the left arm strength is evaluated.

If the left arm gets tired, rest it. Other muscles can be tested since they all get weak. However, the left arm provides a test that allows you to become accustomed to one muscle's perception, and later you can grade the amount of weakness. This amount of weakness roughly correlates with the amount of problem in the circuit.

Now let's review the tests since our last review.

GOOD	BAD	TREATMENT
TEST # 14: Lymph nodes.		
(Under jaw angle).		Detoxification
		Spleen and lymph extract.
		Homeopathic formula.
		Exercise
		Energizer
		Herbs
TEST # 15: Thyroid.		
(Anterior throat).		Check iodine.
		Correct.
		Check hypothalamus.
		Check pituitary
		Thyroid replacement if
		reflex remains abnormal.

TEST # 16: Iodine.

    Between second and third rib just to the right of the sternum.   kelp or organic iodine.

TEST # 17: Vitamin C.
Under middle of left
clavicle.   Vitamin C.

TEST # 18: Bioflavonoids.   Bioflavonoids.

TEST # 19: Calcium.   Calcium

                             Stomach acid helper

                             Vitamin F.

TEST # 20: Vitamin E.   Vitamin E.

THE MAP IS EXPANDING

"Our Body and Our Earth are Made From Starstuff." (Carl Sagan, *Cosmos*)

TEST # 21: VITAMIN F
(Unsaturated fatty acids that are essential)

We must have some fatty compounds to survive. Rich sources are unrancid vegetable oils that are unheated. Some cases of dry skin will improve with Vitamin F. Calcium utilization inside the body is improved when a proper Vitamin F dose is present. The Vitamin F point is located just above the middle collar bone.

If the reflex is wrong, a little safflower, sunflower or other vegetable oil in the mouth will reverse it instantly. This instant reversal of the bad circuit was the first thing to convince me, with a strong, scientific background, to pursue this subject.

The second thing that convinced me was the bottom line—patients were improving for the first time with a variety of illnesses that my drug therapy had only temporized or covered up symptoms. All honest doctors must feel the futility of their treatments on a large variety of non-bacterial illnesses. This method, if

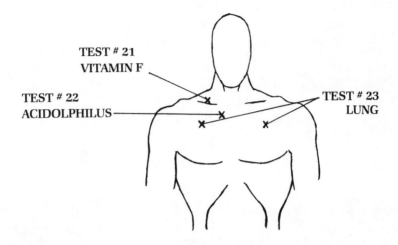

TEST # 21
VITAMIN F

TEST # 22
ACIDOLPHILUS

TEST # 23
LUNG

Figure 23.

physicians allow their minds to open and seek a new data base, will give them alternate choices that expands their therapeutic choices. Many holistic doctors and naturally oriented patients feel resentment toward crisis medicine. I do not share this animosity because of my understanding of the need to deal with many serious and emergency illnesses.

However, there are problems with the current system of established medicine. The prescribing of seven billion tranquilizers attests to this. What we are seeing is an intolerance on the part of scientific medicine to explore more natural methods and to ridicule both the doctors and the public who use such methods. The lay person who is told that "vitamins are unnecessary" and "just eat a balanced diet", rarely goes back to the "scientific" doctor.

When will healers realize that they must quit playing God, get off their pedestals and realize how much wiser the body is than they. There is an increasing desire to return to nutritional methods, more exercise and herbal medicine. This system is both more cost effective and has a superior benefit/risk relationship. I have written a small special section for doctors to clarify my position.

My objective is to allow a healer to realize that he, too, can quickly re-verify what I and hundreds of muscle-testing doctors (kinesiologists) have repeatedly found.

I will have a special area in the appendix that reviews the leading indications for common herbs as suggested by several leading herbalists. Remember that many important drugs are derived originally from herbs, such as digitalis, belladonna and reserpine. Nutrient therapy is also increasing in popularity. These include vitamins, minerals, protein, fiber, essential fats. Muscle energy testing is a revolutionary method that allows you to know about your needs with these natural methods.

TEST # 22: ACIDOPHILUS (LACTOBACILLUS) CIRCUIT

This point is located under the right collar bone in the soft area just next to the breast bone. Patients can get this product from fermented food, yogurt, or buttermilk. Lactobaccillus or acidophilus tablets are available at health stores. Homemade yogurt is one of the best ways to replace this substance. Doctors can write for Bacid or Lactinex from the drug store.

All of these products have one thing in common—to allow a healthier, better balance of bacteria in the colon. This is especially helpful after antibiotic overuse. It can help some cases of excessive rotting of protein (putrification) in the intestine. This causes excessive flatus, abdominal bloating and bad breath. Low stomach acid may contribute to this problem, as can decreased pancreas function. Overeating meat products is the most common reason for this. The old concept of self poisoning (auto-intoxication) is very much a real clinical problem, but is not able to be looked at easily in hospital tests. We will discuss this more when discussing the colon.

We can test the heart with muscle tests, but in many cases of hardening of the arteries, the muscle test is normal. Since the heart is involved with 600,000 deaths in the United States and most heart attacks are taken care of by crisis medicine techniques, I do not feel that a heart muscle test is rewarding and choose to skip it. Instead, I have dedicated a lot of natural ideas to this major killer in my next book on stress.

TEST # 23: LUNG

If you cannot adequately use the air you breathe, a simple muscle test would be to take a deep breath, then test the left arm. If it immediately goes weak, we should recognize the body wisdom is comparing you with your ideal self. A second lung test is to use the looped right hand on a point 1 inches below the collar bone. More precisely, one should divide the collar bone into imaginary thirds. The point is below the junction of the outer one third and the inner two thirds. This Chinese alarm lung-point shows disturbed energy when the lung is not working normally, but sometimes it will be seen to be normal in cases of emphysema if the body has adjusted to it. In other words, if the patient has a mild case and is at rest, then the reflex can be normal. The same is true of asthmatics in between attacks. Thus, we use several tests for the lungs and with over a hundred different problems that affect the lungs, it is best to work with a doctor if significant signs of lung problems exist. These are: (a) Coughing up of blood. (b) Weight loss in a cigarette smoker. (c) Persistent cough. (d) Increasing shortness of breath. A chest X-ray as well as a lung function test are all useful as a follow-up to an abnormal history and muscle test. Remember to use both muscle tests and either one suggests lung disease. The first test (holding your breath after breathing deep) can be useful in showing tobacco users the harm of tobacco. I have surprised many cigarette users by showing how deep breathing weakens them. In such cases, placing the nonfilter end of an unlit cigarette in their mouth, then testing their left arm muscles will show immediate weakness in seventy percent of patients. Hopefully, this will help motivate them to stop tobacco use.

In fact, there are many methods of motivation used today in advising patients what to do. The traditional methods are to play parent and discuss the problem and make recommendations to the patient. Some doctors use hair and blood tests as motivational tool. It is wise to remember that muscle testing can be a motivational tool.

Muscle energy is not only inexpensive and as accurate as any comparative test, but it is the only method by which the patient participates in the test so that he can motivate himself. He can see that an herb or a vitamin is effective immediately. These facts help to reverse two of the most common pitfalls of other methods of chronic medical support-compliance (the patient doesn't do what he is supposed to do) and motivation. Motivation is the key to successful healing.

Reading the iris, for instance, is interesting and helpful, but is not as rewarding in motivating the patient as muscle testing.

Earlier we mentioned that we were dealing with magnetic focal points and closing or checking circuits. Instead of using your right hand or finger, it is possible to use a small straight magnet. A north pole contact that causes the arm to weaken when you test it indicates overactivity of an area. A south pole contact indicates underfunctioning or activity. This originally was worked out by Dr. Albert Roy Davis of Florida. His references are in the appendix.

Section VI

ABDOMEN

TEST # 24: LIVER

An important organ, the liver has many functions. A part of its function can be thought of like an oil filter because pesticides, food additives, chemicals, fumes and drugs generally go to it to be converted into a more agreeable state for the body to eliminate. The liver also stores food overnight in the form of glycogen. This helps prevent early morning low blood sugar. Alcohol misuse will damage the liver and is one of the causes of morning low blood sugar. I will cover blood sugar in more detail in my book on stress.

A disturbed liver can cause a variety of problems and many types of liver problems occur. In cirrhosis, the patient loses his appetite, the abdomen gradually fills with fluid, small spider-like blood vessels appear on the neck and face, certain food fats especially are handled poorly, a bitter or metallic taste in the mouth appears, tiredness increases, the liver edge becomes touchable under the right rib cage and many other signals appear. Though alcohol over-consumption chronically is the most common reason for cirrhosis of the liver to occur, nutritional deficiencies produced at the same time compound the problem. It should be realized that there is a rare familial form of cirrhosis and in adults we see a special type develop after a form of serum hepatitis. Most serum hepatitis cases, however, do not develop into cirrhosis.

Hepatitis is a common condition and is characterized by an inflammation of the liver. Occasionally it will be caused by chemicals, such as methyl ethyl ketone, carbon tetrachloride and other hydrocarbon type products and can be caused by drugs of a large variety of types.

About half of all the cases of infectious hepatitis act like the flu and don't produce jaundice. The other half turn yellow in the whites of the eyes and skin. Itching of the skin, hives, arthritis and kidney conditions can occur in some cases of hepatitis.

In general, relatively "healthy" people with an abnormal liver reflex are having chemical fume exposure, drug use or some leftover energy weakness from a previous liver disease. The liver reflex will often stay abnormal for years after all other tests in the blood have returned to normal, especially after severe hepatitis or mononucleosis. There are many other liver diseases, which include benign and cancerous tumors, cysts, parasites, abscesses and infiltration with infection such as tuberculosis. We cannot always assume that a positive liver test indicates mild liver congestion or residue from some drug. Clinical response is often useful in separating more mild benign problems from more severe problems. If you are not doing well and have a positive liver test, I would suggest you see a holistic physician so he can piece the evidence together with your blood test and clinical history. Sometimes a liver scan is necessary and even a biopsy to confirm the diagnosis more clearly. Usually, however the biopsy is not needed.

Common liver tests on the computer include the bilirubin, albumin and globulin, SGOT, SGPT, and GGTP and alkaline phosophatase. In cirrhosis, the most consistent laboratory test abnormalities are found in the serum protein electrophoresis and consist of a protein bridge between the beta and the gamma globulin fraction, as well as a reduction in albumin. A liver scan is often abnormal also. As the disease progresses, there are more diffuse abnormalities in laboratory testing, including prothrombin time, alkaline phosphatase and sometime bilirubin abnormalities. If there is superimposed alcoholic inflammation, the SGOT and GGTP are usually elevated.

The spleen may get large in more advanced cirrhotic states and the liver has a tendency to shrink and become hard and somewhat painful to touch.

In hepatitis, laboratory tests usually show an elevation of GGTP, SGPT, and SGOT. These elevations are usually quite high and are followed within a few days by increasing bilirubin content and alkaline phosphotase levels. It is necessary to correlate muscle tests with laboratory test and to have proper and thorough followup, because at times, serious and progressive liver disease may occur that is not fully corrected by nutritional methods alone. On the other hand, there are few drugs that are specific for the liver and natural methods are quite useful is assisting the recovery power of the body. In the case of alcohol induced cirrhosis, unless one stops alcohol, nutritional supplementation alone will not be helpful.

In using natural methods to help the liver, recognize that we need to rest it from animal products, but must do so with some degree of intelligence, because patients with cirrhosis and hepatitis require more than average amounts of high quality protein for the healing process. Cirrhotics, who have a lot of fluid in the abdomen which is very protein rich, in fact, may be greatly harmed by fasting attempts and their care should be supervised by a physician interested in these methods. Hepatitis can also be complicated and sometimes fatal.

This book is not being written to discuss the controversies of high dose vitamin C intravenously in assisting hepatitis versus drug therapy, but rather to point out the value of looking at the body and judging that there is something wrong with the liver in the first place, using a simple magnetic test. In many cases of mild drug or chemically induced irritation to the liver, or simply liver congestion related to bile congestion, natural methods are useful in the healing process. This method is also helpful in following hepatitis and mononucleosis, which is sometime accompanied by severe fatigue for periods of months or even years. In such cases, juice fasts of Spirulina cleanses have been useful and the use of a liver flush or cleanser is also helpful. One such flush used for hundreds of years consists of adding to a blender the following ingredients: Two tablespoons of olive oil, the juice of one lemon and the juice of one lime. Sometimes a small clove of garlic is added to the blend, or a pinch of capsicum (cayenne pepper). This blend is either taken in rapidly or utilized one tablespoon every fifteen minutes, should it create too much nausea with being taken all at one time. It is preferable to use an apple juice fast for eight hours prior to the use of this flush, which is best taken at night and followed by the patient sleeping on the right side. A cathartic, such as epsom salts, may be needed the next morning to assist in the passage of the excess bile and debris.

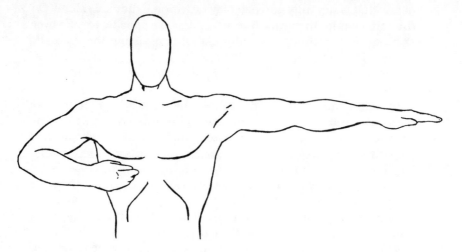

Figure 24.   TEST # 24   LIVER

Performing the liver test is very easy. Just place the open palm side of the right hand under the right breast and test the muscle of the left arm.

Vegetable juices such as celery, carrot, and beet juices are also very helpful with this cleansing. We recommend that you take an herbal laxative a few times during the cleansing. Take the juices every two hours to prevent weakness and take two licorice root capsules every three hours to help prevent low blood sugar. Spring or distilled water should also be used freely during the cleansing. After the initial cleansing, herbal capsules exist to then help keep the liver cleaned out. These include green leaf beet juice tablets, herbal combinations and dandelion. For more damaged livers, the additional use of liver extract or nutritional substance is recommended. (See appendix).

Review

Now, let's review test # 21 through 24.

GOOD	BAD	TREATMENT
TEST # 21: Vitamin F.		Vitamin F.
Above the middle of		Unsaturated fatty acid
the right collar bone.		as capsules or unrancid
		cold pressed oils.
TEST # 22: Acidophilus.		Give yogurt, butter-
Close to the sternum		milk, acidophilus,
under the right collar		liquid or tablets.
bone.		
TEST # 23: Lung.		
1 inch below the		Find the cause.
place where the outer		Beef lung extract.
one third and the inner		Calcium pangamate.
two thirds of the collar		Herbs for mucous
bones meet. It is on		relief.
both sides.		Desert tea.
TEST # 24: Liver.		Find cause.
Just below the right		Detoxify.
breast.		Special "cocktail".
		Bile cleaners, herbs.
		Beef liver extract.
		B-Complex-Vitamin C.

TEST # 25: BILE CIRCUIT

Generally measure how good the bile ducts and gallbladder are working. If the gallbladder has been removed surgically, this test is still frequently abnormal because of the wrong pressures in the common duct system.

The test is done with the looped right hand touching a spot just below the right rib edge, half way between the tip of the breast bone and the side of the body. See illustration.

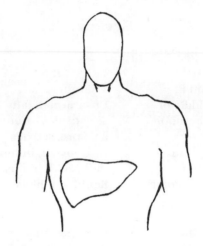

Figure 25.   THE LIVER

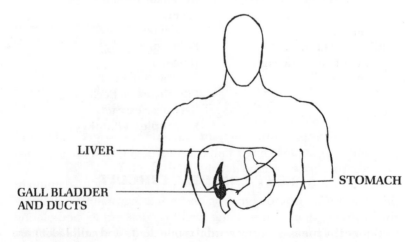

Figure 27.

A bad bile circuit can contribute to evidence that the body is not absorbing fat soluble vitamins well—vitamins A, D, E and K. Also, such patients may have pain in the back and painful spasms in the area that you are testing.

In addition, these people often have gas, bitter taste in the mouth, and are having problems digesting fried or fatty foods.

Treatment is to rule out large gallstones. Natural therapy is similar to that given for the liver. Ox bile, which is available both through health stores and by prescription, is useful in stimulating the flow of bile naturally. It helps to make the bile more thin as well as relax the ducts holding the bile back. Sometimes relaxing herbs or drugs are necessary when there is a lot of spasm involved with the bile ducts of gall bladder. We have witnessed the passage of apparently small gallstones by the use of liver flushes and coffee enemas and semi-fasts as described earlier, and afterward the gall bladder or bile reflex returns to normal.

TEST # 26: STOMACH ACID CIRCUIT

This test will detect the inability of the stomach to produce acid at the time it should. Sometimes this same stomach seems to overmake it at night.

A lack of effective stomach acid doesn't necessarily mean that your stomach isn't making any. Remember in comparing you to how you should be, the best time to get a true reading is after you eat for this particular test.

To test for this point, touch the finger of the looped right hand just under the left rib edge, half way down, between the lower tip of the breast bone and the left side of the body.

To replace stomach acid one can take Betaine HCL, Acidulin (a prescription), glutamic acid or an herbal digestant. Sometimes the stomach acid is not doing well because of bile percolating backwards from the upper intestines. This is especially likely after stomach surgery.

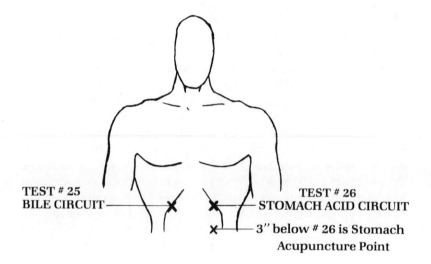

TEST # 25
BILE CIRCUIT————————✗   ✗————TEST # 26
                                                                STOMACH ACID CIRCUIT
                                                                ✗——— 3" below # 26 is Stomach
                                                                              Acupuncture Point

Figure # 26.

TEST # 27: GE VALVE (HIATUS HERNIA) POINT

If this reflex is abnormal it corresponds to a weak valve of the upper stomach. A hiatus hernia will also show up by the method, but about half of all weak valves will not have hiatus hernias with it. In fact, a hiatus hernia with a strong valve can happen and will cause no problems and no weak valve reflex. Treatment depends on the severity of the condition. Manipulation of the back, psoas and diaphragm by a good osteopath or chiropractor are helpful. Sleeping with the head of the bed elevated four to six inches is useful. Beside various drugs, slippery elm, comfrey and aloe vera all have calmed down the problem.

To find this reflex, find a point just to the left of the bottom of the breast bone. It should be in a soft area. Close the reflex with the right hand loop and test the left arm.

This valve problem can cause back pain between the shoulder blades, chest pain that can look like heart pain, a sour taste or fluid running up the mouth, heartburn especially when lying down, sudden severe belly swelling and a lump in the throat.

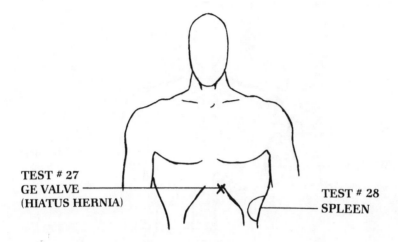

TEST # 27
GE VALVE
(HIATUS HERNIA)

TEST # 28
SPLEEN

Figure # 28.

TEST # 28: SPLEEN

For the purpose of this test, the spleen is a large lymph node. It carries out many other functions as well and plays a role in antibody and immune functions. A positive spleen test by itself can mean an enlarged spleen from a variety of diseases, but usually means a mildly toxic person whose cell wastes are not being adequately removed. Generally this type of person has lymphatic balls (a rosary) in the iris and a positive lymph node circuit. (TEST # 14)

To find this circuit, place the open right hand (palm side) on the left side of the lower rib cage and test the left arm. The spleen lies under the left ribs. Obviously pneumonia in the same area will also give you the same positive test.

To work with this, juice cleansing, proper elimination of kidney, colon and liver and herbs used for "blood purification" and infection are used. Vitamin A and C are helpful and myrrh is especially useful. Spleen and lymph tissue is available as proto-morphogens.

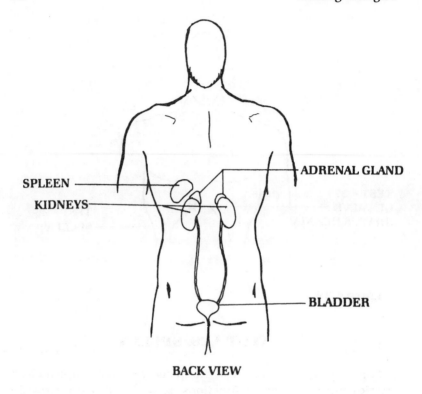

SPLEEN
KIDNEYS
ADRENAL GLAND
BLADDER

BACK VIEW

Figure 30.

TEST #29: KIDNEY

Water soluable wastes are filtered out of our body by the kidneys. This important organ is appreciated when we have a kidney infection, but many times the energy is not right in cases of general swelling (fluid retention). Changes in urinary patterns such as urinating more at night or less during the day, trouble starting the urine or intermittent burning are other signals of kidney or bladder problems. Many times the bladder and kidney circuits will be abnormal together.

To find the kidney circuit, place your right hand (palm side) over your right flank and test the left arm. Now reverse this, and test the right arm with your left palm over your left flank area.

If this test is abnormal, get a urine test to see if you are passing pus, sugar or protein. To help naturally, take appropriate herb combinations, dandelion tea, beef kidney supplement, vitamin C, vitamin A. In prior history of kidney stones, avoid calcium, dairy products and take magnesium supplements.

There is much more to be said about any of the organs because I can discuss with you only a few problem areas. There are 2,000 pages in some reference books on the kidney alone. I am stressing the muscle reflexes here, however, and some things you can do for yourself. I am not diagnosing or prescribing in any person's particular case.

Watch for the bags under the eyes to give you a clue to kidney problems. Another sign is tight rings on the finger when you wake up. Many times the blood test BUN and urine tests are normal and

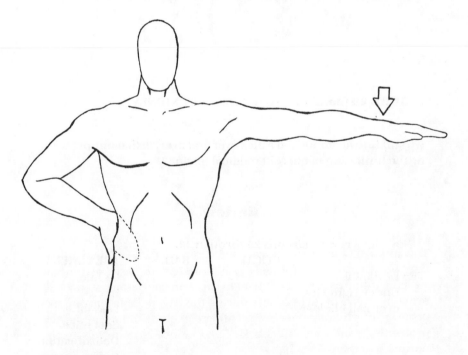

Figure 29.   TEST # 29   **RIGHT KIDNEY**

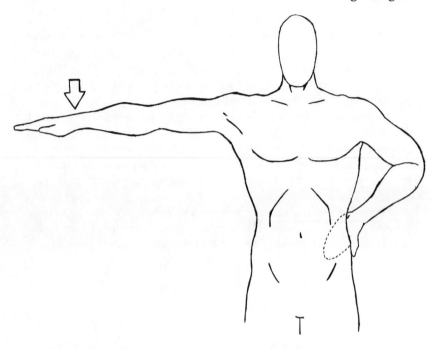

FIGURE 29 (cont'd).   TEST # 29   LEFT KIDNEY

we still find an abnormal reflex over and over. Is that our problem
or the limitation of current medical testing?

Review

Now, let's review circuits 25 through 29.

	GOOD	BAD	TREATMENT
TEST # 25: Bile			Ox bile.
Under right ribs,			Herbs
over gall bladder.			Less fat.
			Beet juice
			Detoxification
			Coffee enema

TEST # 26: Stomach acid.
    Under left ribs,
    midway down
	Betaine
	Glutamic acid
	Detoxification
	Herbs

TEST # 27: GE Valve (hiatus hernia)	Aloe Comfrey Slippery elm Smaller meals Chew well Elevate head of bed
TEST # 28: Spleen.	Detoxification Myrrh Other herbs Vitamin A and C If persists, find cause.
TEST # 29: Kidney.	Dandelion Parsley Juniper Uva ursi Beef Kidney Vitamin A and C

TEST # 30: ADRENAL

This is a key reflex for hypoglycemics, allergic patients and overstressed, chronically tired people. This reflex generally relates to the cortisone producing power of the gland and not the many other aspects of the adrenal. Cortisone type products are naturally made by the body and the amount produced varies according to the time of day and the amount of stress one is under. The four major types of clinical stress are environmental (which includes allergies, infections and physical factors), structural, dietary imbalances and emotional. These will be covered in my next text book on stress.

This reflex tells how well you are reacting to stress compared to your ideal capacity to react to it. Since arthritics having swelling and inflammation in their joints usually have an abnormal adrenal reflex, this suggests that helping natural cortisone production would be generally helpful in such patients. Also, the same holds true in reactive hypoglycemics. Prednisone and other prescribed cortisone type drugs can do this and reverse this reflex. They are subject to giving the patients problems with a variety of side effects. Helping the adrenal gland make the substances naturally does not produce these problems except if the doctor uses a substance called ACTH.

Natural ways to help the gland have a better balance of the main anti-stress hormone is obviously to get to the root of stress and reverse it, supply the gland with adequate nutrition, especially magnesium, Vitamin C and pantothenic acid and avoid refined sugar and flour products. Yucca, licorice root and Mexican wild yams contain products that help the adrenal exhausted patient. Beef adrenal glanular substance can act like a catalytic food for the gland.

In low blood sugar problems, the most common problem is with the liver or adrenal reserves (energies), but sometimes the pancreas is involved.

To do the adrenal reflex, place the right hand (palm portion) on a point two inches up and one and a half inches over from the belly button (umbilicus). Now test the left arm.

If you are using licorice root capsules to help a weak adrenal circuit, it is possible to test the herb in a certain manner, determining first if it is agreeable (compatible) with the person and then determining the specific dose needed.

What I am about to describe applies to all herbs and vitamins and minerals: First, test for compatability. The person holds the bottle full of herbs with his right hand. The left arm is checked for weakness. If weak, *do not* use the substance. If strong, proceed to check the dose required. Note that ideally, the bottle tested should be made from lead-free glass, but in the case of herbs the energies are so strong that even the average plastic container will work. In order to get an accurate compatibility test, the examiner and the patient must be in a neutral mental state and the patient's hypothalamus, pituitary, thymus, iodine and main # 1 switch circuits must be fixed. *This is important*. We will describe the thymus circuit next.

To determine the dose of a substance (not a drug, however), after proving compatibility, open the container and take out one capsule or tablet and place it in the patient's right hand. Then, *close the fingers* over the capsule. The master computer will cause one of two types of reaction. If the left arm goes weak, the computer is registering an underdose. Add another capsule and test again. Continue to add capsules until the arm is suddenly strong. Then add one more and you will see that the arm goes weak again (an overdosage). In the second type of computer response, the brain only records an overdose, not an underdose. Thus, if a person needs three capsules, his arm will stay strong until the fourth capsule is placed in his hand. This determines the dose required at that moment. Often with severe hypoglycemics, five or six licorice root capsules are needed two or three times a day.

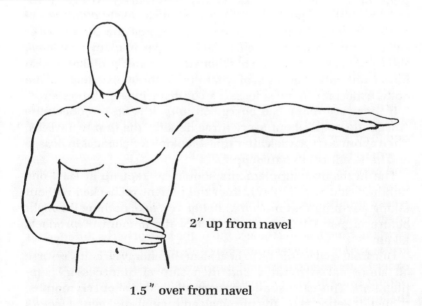

2″ up from navel

1.5″ over from navel

Figure 31. TEST # 30 ADRENAL

TEST # 31: THYMUS (MANGANESE)

Dr. Diamond, in his book "Your Body Doesn't Lie", popularizes the thymus as one of the key reflexes of the body. It is a meeting ground for various energies and an indicator of whether the patient has the power to recover. This reflex is very temperamental and if I find it to be abnormal, I correct it early. It can be helped by certain physical maneuvers (see Diamond's book), by thymus gland extract, manganese or propolis (a special type of Danish beeswax mixed up with tree sap).

The thymus reflex can be found the same way that you follow the steps to locate the iodine reflex (TEST # 16). The only difference is that you use your right hand loop to the center of this area of your breast bone (about two to three inches from the top of the breast bone) where you can usually feel a small ridge or notch in the sternum.

Our goals for supplement support are based on the following philosophy: Nature works slowly but surely—drugs work quickly, but temporarily. The patient most likely didn't get ill overnight and it will take time to overcome the illness. Over reliance on vitamins alone can be improper in many problems, since getting to the bottom of other stress related problems is also important. Shotgunning of vitamins without listening to the body, especially in megadoses, can be disturbing to the system.

If there are many bad energy circuits, it is best to check the "magnetic map" about every three days for the first two weeks. Then about once a week after that—looking for changes in dosage and new reflexes that turn up.

The herbs and supplements should be kept up at least one hundred and twenty days, then the patient rechecked without taking anything that morning. Better yet, take nothing the night before either. Often one can reduce the amount of products taken.

Our final goal would be to heal all of the energy circuits, reverse all abnormal symptoms and then stop all unnecessary supplements. This can usually be accomplished in about six months, though it depends on the physical, emotional and mental factors of the patient and his socio-economic environment.

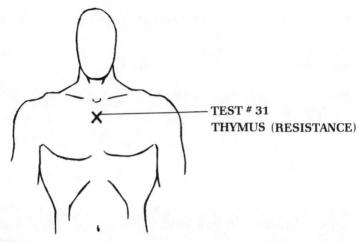

TEST # 31
THYMUS (RESISTANCE)

Figure 32.

By measuring the blueprint magnetically and studying the iris as well as using the traditional medical methods, one can probe deeper into preventing disease or the progression of illness.

I think of the thymus point more like a resistance point. It is highly influenced by mood, sound, light and other frequencies of the electromagnetic spectrum.

TEST # 32: COLON VALVE

This reflex is commonly abnormal due to our refined diet and our loose attitude as to what is "normal" regarding our bowel habits.

Toxic, allergic, migraine and asthmatic people should strive for a mushy bowel after each meal. Herbal laxatives can help to accomplish this, though they may be abused by the unknowledgeable patient. Increasing bulk and water are the two most valuable ways of modifying bowel habits. Bulk can be added as vegetables, bran, psyllium or clay. The dietary method is preferred with psyllium added and initial use of herbal laxative with the goal of making two stools a day. Many patients with one stool a day who are allergic to foods or sensitive to fumes can be benefited by increasing the frequency and size of the stool per day. Be careful of recommending these things to a person with intestinal cramps, colitis or diarrhea tendency.

For that type of patient, investigation of reasons why he may hold things inside emotionally as well as looking honestly for food allergies and providing manipulative care are the most helpful methods. Comfrey, slippery elm and small doses of aloe with gradually increasing doses of fiber can be helpful. Lobelia can help spasm.

To test the colon valve, place the index and middle finger of the right hand on the lower right part of the abdomen (close to the appendix). Now, lift those fingers up toward the left shoulder, pressing moderately into the abdomen. Test the left arm. If weak, it suggests that the valve between the large and small bowel is not closing properly. This can aggravate a tired, toxic feeling. The treatment for this reflex is to improve the clearing of the colon (in severe cases high colonics can be useful) by the measures described above and to consider Lactobaccillus or acidophilus capsules to better balance the intestinal germ content. Chlorophyll liquid or pearls are also helpful.

Proper control of elimination is one of the keys to good health. The basis for this lies in a proper alkaline acid balanced diet (80/20%) for most patients. Rich sources of vegetables and grains are the key. Avoidance of excessive amounts of refined sugar and meat are highly recommended. Only a small amount of adults will tolerate milk safely. For most milk will either be rejected (diarrhea or cramps) or produce mucus.

Mucus production is also aggravated by most milk products, though for some patients, buttermilk, yogurt, Kefir and other fermented milk sources are safe as well as beneficial.

Sometimes the colon (ileocecal) valve is spastic and doesn't allow the digesting food to enter the colon from the small bowel. Usually we see this in cases with very low calcium utilization. In such cases, which are uncommon, the open colon valve reflex will be all right, but if you place the same two fingers two inches higher (above the valve and appendix) and push down and inward toward the appendix, the reflex will cause the left arm to weaken.

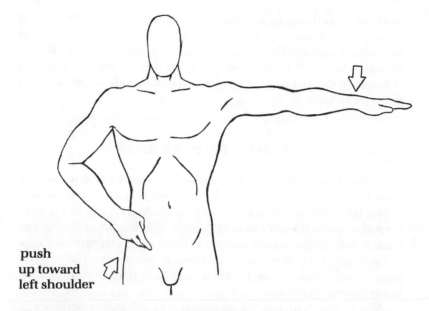

push
up toward
left shoulder

Figure 33. TEST # 32 COLON REFLEX

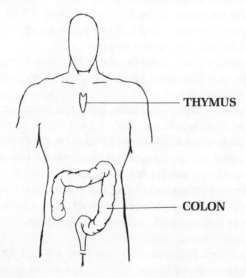

THYMUS

COLON

Figure 34.

This reflex is the *spastic colon valve circuit*. To treat it one must take a good source of calcium, reduce phosphates in the diet (especially soft drinks) and make sure that stomach acid, Vitamin D and Vitamin F circuits are corrected if abnormal. Calcium deficiency can occur in the milk drinker if poor assimilation of the milk occurs.

TEST # 33: PANCREAS

This will be divided into two parts: (a) Pancreas enzyme and (b) overall pancreas function usually pointing to a diabetic tendency.

The pancreas enzyme point is one inch to the right of the belly button. Touch it with the middle right finger pad of the looped right hand. If abnormal, reduce refined carbohydrate and total animal product load. Add pancreatic enzymes. Often such patients complain of gas, bloating, vague stomach discomfort and sometimes diarrhea.

Alcohol can damage the pancreas and this reflex becomes of major importance if present in alcohol abusers.

I feel that digestive help should be given specifically. The three main upper digestive circuits to check then are: (a) Stomach acid. (b) Bile circuit. (c) Pancreatic enzyme circuit.

The main pancreatic circuit must be tested by a special muscle test. The latissimus dorsi muscle correlates with the pancreas and should be tested directly.

To test this muscle, which correlates with the pancreas, the tester lightly grasps the patient's wrist and explains what he is about to do first. "On the count of three, I will try to pull your arm away from your body. I will pull outward, but slightly forward at the same time. You should resist me with all your might. One. Two. Three." Both arms should be tested and if either one is weak and is corrected by pancreas glandular product, then an inherent pancreatic weakness is suggested. Further blood sugars are often suggested at this point. (See illustration).

If the pancreas reflex is abnormal, ask the patient about a diabetic history, personally or in the family. Was the person born weighing more than nine pounds? (Many of these people will become diabetic). Is there a definite history of low blood sugar?

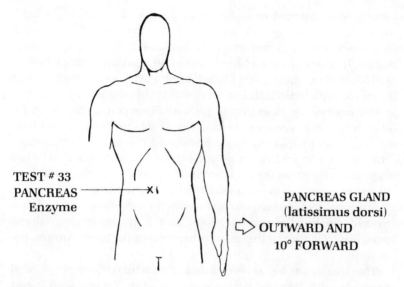

TEST # 33
PANCREAS
Enzyme

PANCREAS GLAND
(latissimus dorsi)
OUTWARD AND
10° FORWARD

Figure 35.

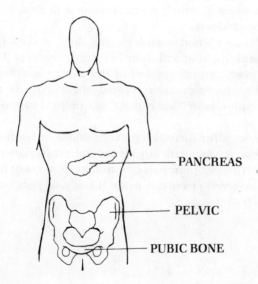

PANCREAS

PELVIC

PUBIC BONE

Figure 37.

About fifty percent of hypoglycemics are destined to become diabetic. Some doctors study diabetes by way of a glucose tolerance test, but not even all nutritional doctors use it any more. It is wise to get a blood sugar one hour after lunch before age 55, and two hours after lunch after age 55, as a screening test to rule out diabetes if the pancreas test is abnormal.

Remember, by doing these tests and correcting the magnetic energy circuit, you are picking up problems before the blood testing is abnormal, so sugar imbalance is a later stage. Dietary changes, herbs and vitamins and minerals can do the most good as preventive measures, so the vital importance of this system of measurement can act as a valuable tool in everyone's home.

Another problem we often see with the pre-diabetic is delayed wound healing, recurrent boils and a tendency for edema (swelling). Of course there are other causes for these complaints as well.

The treatment for severe diabetes, of which there are several types, is with insulin. If you are on insulin, do not stop it and convert over to something else. Fatal consequences may occur. There are natural measures that can help most diabetics, however. In some cases, with the guidance of a doctor, insulin can be reduced or stopped.

Several herbs* have a blood sugar lowering ability and adequate amounts of chromium, zinc and vitamin C can be helpful. Fiber, such as wheat, bran and conversion of the diet to a high fiber moderate protein, low fat, zero refined sugar type is most helpful. Pancreas glandular food extract* is a helpful supporting substance.

There are homeopathic formulas that are said to be useful, but they must be prescribed specifically for the individual patient.

The patient with a weak pancreas circuit may or may not have a weak pancreas enzyme circuit. A prior history of pancreatitis usually weakens both.

*See Appendix.

TEST # 34: MAGNESIUM

The magnesium point is one inch below the belly button. Touch it the same way you tested the pancreas enzyme circuit.

Magnesium is a vital element important in working with hundreds of enzymes in your body. Energy enzymes for instance, are dependent on magnesium. If there is a weak reflex, use magnesium supplement or foods rich in magnesium. It is not possible to go into greater detail regarding nutrition in this type of book, since we are covering another subject of equal or even greater importance—a way of learning how to explore the wisdom of the body.

Magnesium decrease may be temporary or chronic. Diuretics can aggravate potassium and magnesium loss and one can also find such loss in alcohol users, with other liver diseases, with chronic diarrhea or stool loss, such as stomach drainage. Refer back to the second circuit, the one showing right or left brain function predominance. In a magnesium person (where the potassium and calcium circuits test strong), we usually find a tired or nervous individual who is difficult to improve. They are often intermittently switched (circuit # 1) and often oscillate between left and right brain predominance. In simple language, their nervous system is electrically unstable.

TEST # 35: OVARY

Feel the upper part of your pelvic bone. Now follow until it stops. This front part of the iliac crest is called the anterior superior iliac spine. One inch inward (toward the middle of the belly) on each side is the ovary circuit. If the ovaries are not functioning up to par, or if they are inflamed, the reflex will be abnormal. It will also pick up most cases of cysts. Sometimes, however, cysts and tumors will not register on magnetic circuits, especially if the tumor tissue is similar to the normal tissue. This applies to tumors in other areas as well. If the ovaries have been removed, you will not get an abnormal response in most cases. There is no ovary to give such a response. The same applies to kidneys or other parts that are removed. Ovaries must be treated according to the cause of the problem. Estrogen is helpful in some cases where hot flashes and change of life problems exist. This is especially true in young women with surgically removed ovaries. High dose Vitamin E and certain herbs as well as ovarian extract (a food concentrate) can be used instead of estrogen in many cases. Ovarian cysts and infection must be treated by additional methods in many cases.

TEST # 36: BLADDER

Feel the tummy and move the hand down until you run into the pubic bone. Just above this bone in the midline is the bladder

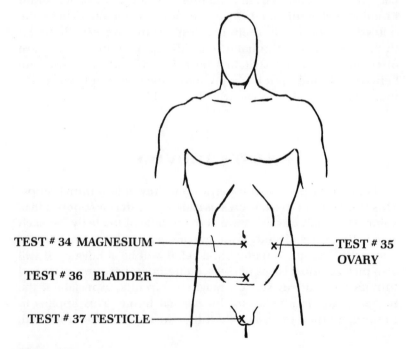

TEST # 34 MAGNESIUM

TEST # 36 BLADDER

TEST # 37 TESTICLE

TEST # 35
OVARY

Figure 36.

point. Close the circuit with the right middle finger pad of the looped right hand, just as in the ovarian, magnesium and other "points" circuits.

There are many bladder disturbances: Tumors, cysts, stones, infection, narrow opening and ulcers, to name a few. Certain herbs can help irritation of the bladder*. Certain foods can aggravate bed wetting in fifty percent of cases. (Milk, chocolate, cola, citrus, corn and wheat). Some cases of recurrent cystitis *without infection* are also aggravated by foods in adults. Wheat is especially prone to do this. A detailed discussion of tracking down these allergies is found in my next book on stress.

TEST # 37: TESTICLE CIRCUIT

The man places his right fingers on the testicles and if the left arm goes weak, then evaluation of why is required. If impotence is present, this reflex can indicate if a physical factor (male menopause, diabetes, arteriosclerosis) is present. If it is strong, then impotence is probably of emotional origin. Male hormone is used in some of these nonemotional caused cases. Chelation therapy is said to help at times, and certain glandular tissue (orchic) and herbs* are useful. In many cases, however, the impotence has an emotional basis and can definitely be helped by a combination of nutritional and emotional therapy where the nerve or circulation is not permanently damaged.

TEST # 38: BLOOD VESSEL INSTABILITY

(hypertensive tendency circuit)

Draw in the cheeks between the teeth. If the left arm goes weak, it suggests that the blood pressure should be evaluated. High blood pressure is a "silent killer" and, contrary to popular opinion, is not supposed to go higher as you get older. If it is high,

*See appendix.

there may be an inner cause for it. Ten percent of the cases have a curable reason. Ninety percent need either drugs, stress reduction, biofeedback, manipulation and/or herbs. Garlic and capsicum are useful in mild to moderate cases. Reduction of salt is helpful in many cases, and herbs to help the nerves (nervines) and kidneys are useful in these cases*.

In more severe caes, drugs may be needed. This test is usually abnormal with cases of high blood pressure and with cases where the blood pressure goes up with stress, even if the pressure is normal at the time it is checked. Repeated checking will find it. Home blood pressure equipment is available from many stores and medical supply houses.

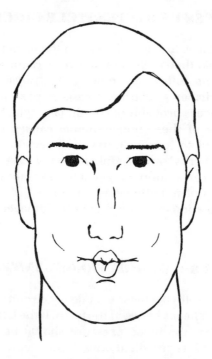

Figure 38.   TEST # 38   BLOOD VESSEL TEST

*See Appendix.

TEST # 39: COLITIS CIRCUIT

The lower intestine often are the target of emotional conflict and allergies. This is especially true of individuals who hold it in. Many times this runs in families. Sometimes the same condition is totally or partially aggravated by specific foods. Any food can cause this. "One man's meat is another man's poison". The small bowel circuit is found one and one half inch above the bladder point (about halfway between the magnesium point and the bladder point). Touch it the same way as for the bladder circuit. The small bowel circuit can be aggravated by anything that affects the small bowel, not just colitis. Now, touch the area of the sigmoid colon (lower left part of the belly with the second, third

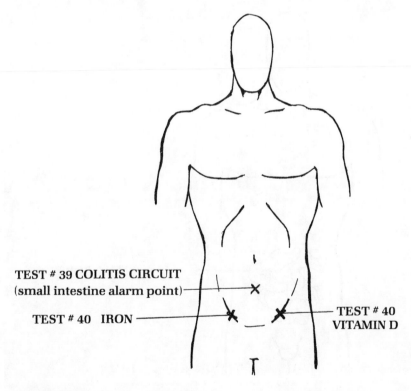

TEST # 39 COLITIS CIRCUIT
(small intestine alarm point)

TEST # 40   IRON

TEST # 40
VITAMIN D

Figure 39.

and fourth fingers of the right hand), and if both small bowel and the sigmoid circuits are abnormal, spastic colitis is usually the cause. Infections, ulcerative and granulomatous colitis can also cause this, though more rarely. Again the reflexes are nonspecific guides that should be followed by asking questions. The reflexes somtimes are abnormal *before* physical symptoms.

Spastic colitis patients usually have cramping and either constipation or diarrhea tendencies under excessive emotions or with the wrong food. The stool can be narrow and ribbon-like. Cancer of the colon may show up as an abnormal circuit if the cancer is in the sigmoid, but may not if it is in some other area of the colon. If the test is positive in the absence of symptoms, ask your doctor about a hemoccult test. This test screens for tumors.

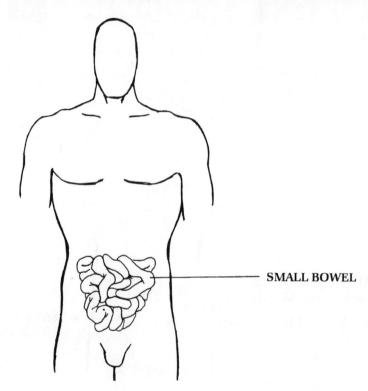

SMALL BOWEL

Figure 40.

Note that thus far, muscle testing is not only helping serve as an early warning system to find and prevent problems, but also serves as a guide to spot many cases of killer diseases at a stage when modern medical care has a better chance to diagnose and "cure".

TEST # 40: GROIN

Halfway between the pubic bone and the front tip of the pelvic bone (anterior superior spine) lies our next reflex. On the right side, it suggests a decrease of iron and on the left side, a lack of vitamin D.

It may indicate an excess of these elements as well, but I am not yet sure of this personally. Every reflex here has been checked out by myself several hundred of times. I feel that these circuits usually indicate underactivity or disordered activity in the respective organ or nutrient circuit.

Review

Now, let's review the last ten circuits:

	GOOD	BAD	TREATMENT
TEST # 30: Adrenal. Two inches up and one and a half inches on either side of the umbilicus.			Licorice root, wild Mexican yam, Vitamin C, Pantothenic acid manganese, magnesium, B-Complex, adrenal glandular support.
TEST # 31: Thymus. In the middle of the Notch (angle of Louis) about two inches down from the top of the breast bone			Thymus extract Manganese Propolis, bee pollen.
TEST # 32: Colon Valve. (Open). Push two fingers in the area of the appendix, up toward the shoulder.			Acidophilus, Chlorophyll, Fiber, good bowel habits, herbs.

(Closed). Push two fingers
downward toward the
appendix

Calcium, HCL
replacement.

TEST # 33: Pancreas.

Pancreas enzyme—one inch
to the right of the belly
button (umbilicus).

Pancreas enzyme

Pancreas-overall-test
latissiumus dorsi, pull
arm outward under
resistance and look for
weakness.

Dietary changes, in-
vestigate for diabetes
Pancreas glandular extract
Zinc, Vitamin C, chromium,
Potassium if deficient.

TEST # 34: Magnesium.
One inch below the
umbilicus.

Magnesium from natural
sources.

TEST # 35: Ovary.
One inch medial
(toward the midline)
from the front tip of
the pelvic bone on
both sides—check both.

Estrogen, herbs, ov-
arian substance

TEST # 36: Bladder
Just above the pubic
bone in the midline

Herbs
Urine check
Treat infection
Food allergies
Dilate opening as needed.

TEST # 37: Testicle.
Holding the testicle.

Orchic tissue.
Males hormone, emotional
help, better elimination
and nutrition.
Chelation (as needed)

TEST # 38: Blood vessel
instability.
Draw in soft part of
cheeks inward between
outer teeth

Check blood pressure,
Herbs, reduce sugar and
salt, manipulation.

TEST # 39: Colitis.
    Small bowel—halfway
    between the bladder and
    magnesium circuits.
    Sigmoid colon.
    Three fingers on the
    left lower abdomen.

Herbs.
Manipulation, fiber.
Emotional help.

Herbs, hemoccult, rule
out more serious problems.

TEST # 40: Groin.
    Half way between pubes
    and anterior spine of
    Pelvis.
    Right side
    Left Side

Iron
Vitamin D

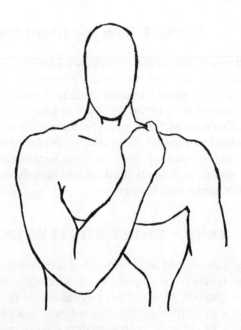

Figure 41. TEST # 41   VITAMIN A

TEST # 41: VITAMIN A

Bring your right arm around in front of you, and with the middle finger pad (hand looped) touch the top of the left shoulder above the middle of the collar bone. It may be hard to reach because this point is on the top of the trapezius muscle. The spot is half way between the tip of the shoulder joint and the area where the neck starts.

Vitamin A is helpful in restoring night blindness, certain cases of dry skin and damaged linings such as the sinus back toward normal. In very high dose, it can be toxic (like Vitamin D). People with lower amounts of vitamin A in the blood stream are at a higher risk of cancer. Are you getting adequate yellow and green vegetables or fish sources?

TEST # 42: B-COMPLEX

Though some preliminary work exists for the different B vitamins with this testing method, the re-verification has not proceeded long enough for me to share these with you. Instead, a general B-Complex point has been found at the tip of the tongue. If you test weak while touching this spot with the looped right middle finger pad, it should be corrected immediately if B-Complex is placed in the mouth. One can even test for each of the B vitamins separately using this point, but that would be time consuming and usually unnecessary, since B-Complex works best in harmony.

TEST # 43: SURROGATE TESTING

By now you should appreciate that a biologic energy surrounds the body. It has been found that this energy can be transferred from one person to another. Laying on of hands and polarity healing are examples of this. We can use this fact in testing very weak, very ill or very young patients who cannot directly co-operate with us in muscle testing.

First, you need someone to help who has a strong test in question, or perhaps all of his muscle tests will be strong (a rarity). You can correct his weak areas with supplements or whatever is required before you go on. Now, have this subject (the weak patient who cannot be tested) hold onto your helper's waist with one hand on either side. Usually the helper stands in front of the seated or lying patient. When contact is made, you will see that some reflexes previously strong in the helper become weak only when the patient makes contact. In this way, it is possible to create a magnetic map of one person via another. Remember, you cannot get a valid test if the helper has bad reflexes to begin with. They must be corrected.

There are still other reflexes to tap the wisdom of the body, but I feel that the present circuits can serve as an adequate "map". At first, learning these reflexes may seem difficult, but with time the entire map can be done rapidly and accurately in three or four minutes. Like learning to play a musical instrument or learning to type, your skill is directly proportional to your enthusiasm and repetition of the process.

Before leaving this subject, I wish to pass on one other tip to help you. How can you determine if a substance is agreeable or disagreeable? With so many health oriented books being written, it is important for one to have the capacity for the body itself to choose that which offends it. To check a food, simply put a small amount in your mouth and check your left arm for muscle strength. If weak, it is important to appreciate that the weakening food should be studied to see if it is really causing any true clinical problems.

Food intolerances are not always allergies and can cause an aggravation of any problem in the problem. Any part of the body can be affected including the brain, aggravating anxiety, depression, convulsions, psychosis. Hypoglycemia, some arthritis, migraine, and skin problems are frequently aggravated by specific foods. Remember, one man's meat is another man's poison. This rule is more important than what one nutritionist or another says generally. They are referring to groups of people. You are not necessarily in that group. Some doctors perform the test by merely putting the food (directly or an extract in a glass bottle) in the patient's hand and then testing the opposite arm. My companion book will show methods of separating out the truly hidden culprits from the foods that mildly weaken you with no other problems.

Vitamins are made from a variety of substances and sometimes they are not agreeable. Testing a vitamin is a good idea. In fact, test all your supplements (they can be calculated as to exact dosage by following the rules expressed earlier in this book). This applies to vitamins, minerals, glandulars and herbs.

About twelve percent of patients that I have seen appear to have difficulties in a deeper electrical system, related to the original Chinese acupuncture system. A general screening test to find out if there is a significant electrical problem in this area is to correct all the switch circuits which presumably will automatically correct the minor secondary acupuncture problems, leaving only the major acupuncture disturbances still present. If you make an amplification loop with your right hand, placing the middle finger pad directly over the umbilicus, then if the left arm goes weak, you probably have an acupuncture circuit abnormality. Finding acupuncture circuits by muscle testing is possible and so is correcting them, using acupressure. Many times RNA or thymus will help to reverse the circuits without the need for acupressure. Sometimes a specific protomorphogen or glandular replacement will correct a specific circuit. The lung glandular for an insufficient lung meridian, for example. It is possible to be very complicated in discussing acupuncture because of the many laws governing the traditional method of using this healing art.

Since only a minority of problems in our patients can be tracked down to having a persisitent acupuncture problem, and since acupressure is often only temporarily helpful in correcting the defect, we do not choose to make the list more complicated by various laws or rituals or methods employing this noble and ancient healing art. If, however, you have corrected all the other circuits and your acupuncture screening circuit is repeatedly positive, then I would suggest that you inquire further by seeking qualified professional help. At times the diamond gait mentioned in Dr. Diamond's book "Your Body Doesn't Lie" will correct these acupuncture circuits automatically. You may have to repeat it to get it to work, however. This walk, coincidentally, is very effective in reducing many abnormal body circuits and not just those of the acupuncture "layer". I do not choose to recommend the walk, initially, however, so that more accurate diagnostic information can be acquired. The walking may cover up some of the reflexes and we are not sure how long they will stay away otherwise. We do recommend the walk, however, after you have corrected your major defects and circuits and are on the way to uncovering the basic stresses that created the problem to begin with. In my opinion, diamond gait is an excellent breathing and balancing experience to improve the life energy and the life force.

Visualizing light and colors is a well known tool enhancing relaxation in mediation therapy. It is not necessary to do this portion while doing the Diamond gait, but if it comes easy to you, and it usually does with practice, then by all means do it. Practicing a relaxed, meditative technique which is followed by creative visualization to accomplish specific goals is one of the most healing experiences for relaxing and de-stressing individuals known, and has been used for thousands of years for that purpose.

Section Section VII

CIRCUITS

(Clinical Considerations)

Defects in certain tests may indicate a certain pattern or problems. A holistic-oriented doctor will usually consider these automatically and combine the knowledge obtained with other tests such as blood tests and iris or hair tests.

Let's consider a few examples:

A 28 year old patient named Tom complained of fatigue, dry skin and intermittent loose stools. Parasite involvement and anemia were ruled out by testing.

Muscle energy testing indicated a pancreatic enzyme abnormality, although the general pancreas testing was normal. The bile circuit was also abnormal. When both bile flow and pancreas enzymes are less than adequate, various digestive problems may arise and yet be virtually impossible to discover by the usual tests in a hospital. Special extensive medical testing can pick some of these cases up, but this simple method, which is *free* can allow a person to go on a clinical trial of bile salts and pancreas enzymes.

In Tom's case, his symptoms cleared up dramatically and the bile salts were only needed temporarily.

When the bile circuit is abnormal, always check for fat soluable vitamins, A, D, E, and K. Appropriate bile flow is helpful for their absorption.

With Tom, the A, D, and E points were all abnormal and the use of cod liver oil (a source of natural A and D) and supplemental E were helpful in improving his skin dryness. A vitamin F abnormality is also found in some cases of liver or bile flow problems.

To review again, the Vitamin A point is located by placing the looped hand (middle finger pad) on a spot half way between the bottom of the neck and the tip of the shoulder on the left side.

Sally was a hypoglycemic who suffered from headaches, dizziness, mental confusion and tiredness. She craved sweets. There was no history of diabetes in her family.

(Hypoglycemics usually have one or more of the following abnormal circuits: (a) Liver, especially in people with previous liver disease, on drug therapy or alcohol users. (b) Pancreas, especially if diabetes is or will appear. (c) Adrenal, especially in the allergic or toxic patients or those under a lot of stress.)

In Sally's case, the liver was all right, but the pancreas and adrenal circuits were abnormal. We tested her for diabetes and found she did have a pattern consistent with early diabetes.

Sally teaches us that just because the family history is apparently negative for diabetes does not exclude the possibility that it is present in the patient, or overlooked in the family as well.

We treated Sally with a high fiber, low fat, zero refined sugar diet and supported the adrenal temporarily with water soluable vitamins and corrected the symptoms quickly with calcium and licorice root. Licorice root gives cortisone-type assistance without the problems of the actual cortisone drug.

Eileen was an elderly white female who had comlained of stomach spasm, nervousness and leg cramps at night. She didn't drink milk and took a calcium supplement from the pharmacy.

When I checked her, the calcium point was off, indicating the calcium was going through her like chalk. The stomach acid point was abnormal and Betaine Hydrochloride with pepsin was given to her to take before meals along with her calcium. In 48 hours she showed a reversal of all problems and also reported better resting at night and better concentration.

Eileen is typical of patients of all ages with calcium deficiency. In many of these people, hydrochloric acid is not made appropriately to help dissolve or ionize the calcium.

Now, stomach acid deficiency is one of the causes of heartburn, gas and bloatiness, but may exist with no symptoms. If giving Betaine to those patients who show a need (by the stomach reflex and/or symptoms) causes worse heartburn, it is best to stop this substance and seek medical help to rule out tumors or more serious problems. If a more serious problem is eliminated, it suggests that the lower esophagus (the most common site of heartburn), stomach or duodenum is raw or inflamed.

A calming herb is helpful in these cases to give the upper intestine and stomach a chance to heal. Comfrey, aloe, cabbage and slippery elm are all useful at that point and an herbal calcium not requiring stomach acid can be substituted (horsetail, couch-grass, alfalfa).

Other reflexes that should be corrected when a patient taking calcium still has a bad calcium circuit: (a) Vitamin F, corrected with unrancid cold pressed oil. (b) Vitamin D, correct with more sunshine and/or a natural vitamin D source.

Diet changes are often needed to ensure continued balance of magnetic reflexes. In Eileen's case, soft drinks which she was fond of, were stopped, since they contained a high load of phosphate. Phosphorus loads may decrease the effective utilizaiton of calcium.

People with low calcium often are left-hemisphere dominant, heavy meat-eaters, with alkaline stools (putrefying meat), have allergic tendencies and are edgy or nervous.

The blood calcium is often low normal in these people, but the hair calcium is often high (in theory abnormal calcium load is coming from the bone to the hair). In the iris they often have cramp rings (nerve rings).

Philip was a 9 year old boy with fatigue, pale face, growing pains and periodic stomach pains and headaches.

Since children like to play with games, it is fun and easy to show them that muscle testing works and MOTIVATE them to change.

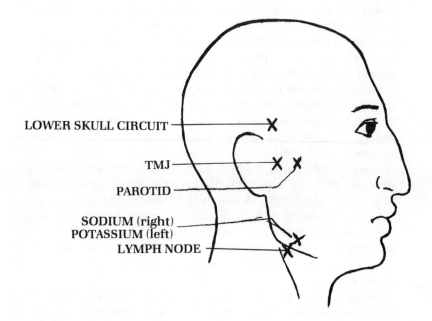

LOWER SKULL CIRCUIT

TMJ

PAROTID

SODIUM (right)
POTASSIUM (left)
LYMPH NODE

In fact, this is the best method I have found to MOTIVATE adults and children alike to making a change.

Philip's case was chosen because we felt by his symptoms that he had a food allergy. His switch circuit (circuit # 1), was reversed. This was corrected by having him chew and swallow an RNA tablet. We then had him hold small round unleaded glass bottles containing a variety of food and chemical substances. The actual foods would have worked nearly as well, but we have testing bottles in the office. Milk, chocolate and wheat caused him to get weak immediately. He was tested for these items by other methods to verify that they caused problems and by avoiding these foods, *all* of his symptoms disappeared.

When testing a substance by this method, make sure that all five major switch circuits are correct first. If you do not, you often get backward and erratic information. The five circuits are the #1 switch circuit, the iodine, the thymus, the hypothalamus and the pituitary circuits.

Sometimes you can be fooled when testing by this method because of the following problems: (a) If you place a chemical in a round glass, small bottle (like an unleaded dropper bottle) it will show a negative result in a few cases that will turn positive if you uncap the bottle and let them smell the fumes. (b) To be weak to a chemical is not the same as being allergic to it. (The body is just expressing that it is disagreeable to the system and has caused a shock or stress). The same applies to foods. (c) Sometimes a food will appear safe with this test, but, in fact, cause problems a few hours later. The body in this case is reacting to some breakdown product of the additive or the food. (d) Foods and chemicals that cause weakness with this test may not cause any clinical symptoms when directly challenged by the patient. (It merely shows that the body can record bad vibes before it causes any obvious problems).

Section VIII

APPENDIX

Sources of Nutritional Physicians

International Academy of Preventive Medicine, Suite 467, 34 Corporate Woods, 10950 Grandview, Overland Park, Kansas 66210

The American Holistic Medical Association, contact C. Norman Shealy, M.D., Ph.D., Route 2, Welch Coulee, LaCrosse, Wisconsin 54601

International College of Applied Kinesiology 542 Michigan Boulevard, Detroit, Michigan 48226

The Association of Research and Enlightenment, P.O. Box 595, Virginia Beach, Virginia 23451

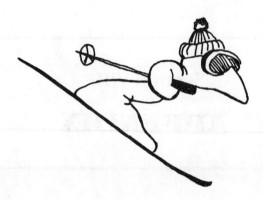

Herbs

Herbs are nature's food for healing. Throughout the ages the common people resorted to herbal remedies to help themselves. Both the Old and New Testament describe faith and herbs as the main healing modes. A resurgence of interest in herbs is arising, especially since high-quality, encapsulated herbs have become widely available. Various herbal combinations are present to increase the power and efficiency of the products.

The following list of herbs and their medicinal value was compiled from various herbalists, including Christopher, Griffin, Ritchason and Heinerman.

Historic Uses of Nature's Herbs

ALFALFA—For pituitary gland, arthritis, chlorophyll, high nutritive, alkalizes body rapidly, detoxifies body and liver.

BARBERRY BARK—Laxative, typhoid, jaundice, improves appetite.

BAYBERRY—Has been used for congestion in the nose and sinuses. It is extremely good for all female organs.

BEE POLLEN-Energy food and allergies.

BLACK COHOSH—Female estrogen, menstrual cramps, high blood pressure, spinal meningitis, poisonous bites, relieves childbirth pain at delivery.

BLACK WALNUT—cleanses parasites, TB, expels tapeworms, diarrhea.

BLESSED THISTLE—Strengthens the heart and lungs, takes oxygen to the brain.

BLUE COHOSH—Regulates menstrual flow, makes childbirth easier, whooping cough, bronchial mucus, palpitations, high blood pressure and spasms.

BUCKTHORN—Rheumatism, gout, dropsy, skin disease.

BURDOCK—Blood purifier, diuretic.

CACTUS—Has been used for arthritis.

CAPSICUM—Catalyst for all herbs, stops internal bleeding, circulation, use with Lobelia for nerves. Use as a stimulant for healing.

CASCARA SAGRADA—Chronic constipation, gallstones, increases secretion of bile.

CATNIP—Convulsions in children, sleep aid, soothing to nerves, insanity.

CHAMOMILE—Nerves, toothache, helps to stop smoking, alcohol, muscle pain.

CHAPARRAL—Cleanser, arthritis, blood purifier, acne and boils.

CHICKWEED—Bronchial cleanser, eats carbohydrates (fat), deafness, peritonitis.

COMFREY ROOT—Blood cleanser, ulcers, stomach, kidneys bowel.

CORNSILK—Kidney and bladder problems, prostate gland, for painful urination.

DAMIANA—Diuretic, kidney and bladder, iron anemia, gout, high in calcium and other vitamins and minerals.

EYEBRIGHT—Aids the vision, the uppermost parts of the throat as far as the windpipe.

FENNEL—Has been used to eliminate colic in babies, helps kill appetite, aids in digestion when uric acid is the problem.

FENUGREEK—Healing, fevers, lubricates the intestines, useful for the eyes.

GARLIC—has been used to emulsify the cholesterol and loosen it from the arterial walls. Effective in arresting intestinal putrefaction and infection.

GINGER—Stimulates circulation (pelvic area), gas, indigestion, paralysis of the tongue.

GINSENG—Male hormone, longevity, prostate, stomach problems.

GOLDEN SEAL—Antibiotic, acts as an insulin, cleanser, morning sickness, cure-all type herb.

GOTU KOLA—Mental troubles, blood pressure, energy, depression, longevity, strengthens the heart, memory and brain, nervous breakdown.

GRAPEVINE—Excellent for dropsy, chronic dysentery, diarrhea, gallstones, kidney stones.

HAWTHORNE—Has been used to dilate the coronary blood vessels in a mild way and restore the heart muscle wall.

HO SHOU-WU—Impotency, longevity. Has been used for tumors, piles, menstrual problems, colds and diarrhea.

HOPS—Insomnia, restlessness, shock, decreases the desire for alcohol.

HORSETAIL—Has been used as a diuretic, heavy in silica, helps with kidney stones.

JUNIPER BERRIES—Has been used for kidney or bladder problems relating to pancreas and adrenal glands. Works well for dropsy and leucorrhea.

KELP—Thyroid, arteries, nails, hair falling out, cleanses radiation from body.

LICORICE ROOT—Natural cortisone, hypoglycemia, adrenal glands, stress, voice, colds.

LOBELIA—Strong relaxant, emetic in large amounts, asthma, angina pectoris, epilepsy, strengthens muscle action, weak heart, use with Capsicum.

MARSHMALLOW—Has been used to bathe sore and inflamed eyes, bladder and kidney problems.

MULLEIN—Has been used for breathing problems, hay fever, pain killer, glandular swelling.

MYRRH GUM—Has been used as an antiseptic, healing, also used for halitosis (bad breath).

PAPAYA MINT—Has great enzyme action for digestion of foods, fats, starches and carbohydrates as well as protein. Gas or sour stomach.

PARSLEY—Known to be high in vitamin B and potassium. Also contains a substance in which tumorous cells cannot multiply.

PASSION FLOWER—Sedative, menopause, headache, neuralgia, hysteria, high blood pressure caused by mental problems.

PEACH BARK—Bladder, uterine troubles, jaundice, inflammation of the abdomen.

PSYLLIUM—Excellent colon cleanser, creates bulk, anti-intoxication.

RED CLOVER—Blood purifer, relaxes the nerves and entire system.

RED RASPBERRY—Dysentery, diarrhea, strengthens uterine walls prior to childbirth.

REDMOND CLAY—Minerals, cleanses worms from intestinal tract, skin disorders, acne.

ROSEHIPS—Has been used as an infection fighter. Also used as a stress herb.

ROSEMARY—Used to prevent baldness, threatened miscarriage, obesity, nightmares. Also used for high blood pressure.

SAFFLOWER—Natural hydrochloric acid (utilizes sugar of fruits an oils), skin disease, neutralizes uric acid, gout, hypo- and hyperglycemia.

SAGE—Used to prevent night sweats, expel worms in children and adults, stops bleeding of wounds and cleans old ulcers and sores.

SARSAPARILLA—Male hormone, rheumatism, gout, psoriasis, antidote for poison.

SAW PALMETTO BERRIES—Has been used for alcoholism, asthma, bladder, colds, bronchitis, diabetes, frigidity, glands, prostate. Has helped underweight people to gain weight. It has also been used to help enlarge small breasts.

SCULLCAP—Nerve tonic, rabies, hysteria, migraines, strengthens heart.

SLIPPERY ELM—Inflamed mucous membranes of the stomach, bowels, kidneys.

THYME—Supressed menstruation, nerves, colic, gas.

UVA URSI—Diabetes, kidneys, hemorrhoids, spleen, liver, pancreas, gonorrhea.

VALERIAN ROOT—Nervous disorders, headache, muscle twitching, spasms, promotes sleep.

WHITE OAK BARK—Use in douches and enemas, varicose veins, loose teeth, bladder, goiter, gallstones, kidney stones, fever and sores.

WOOD BETONY—Indigestion, stomach cramps, worms, jaundice, Parkinson's disease.

YARROW—Used in diarrhea, has soothing and healing action on mucous membranes.

YELLOW DOCK—Blood purifier, cleanser, acne, high in iron, tones the entire system.

YUCCA—Has been used for rheumatoid and osteoid forms of arthritis.

BIBLIOGRAPHY

AND
SUGGESTED READING LIST

IRIDOLOGY AND HERBS:

Kriege, Theodor. *Fundamental Basis of Iris Diagnosis*. 1201 High
    Road, Chadwell Heath, Romford RM6 4DH, Essex: L. N. Fowler
    and Company, Ltd.
Kloss, Jethro. *Back to Eden*. Santa Barbara, California: Lifeline
    Books, 1975.
Lust, John. *The Herb Book*. Simis Valley, California: Benedict-
    Lust Publications, 1974.
*Heinerman, John. *Science of Herbal Medicine*. 1979.
*Griffin, La Dean. *Is Any Sick Among You?* 1974.
*Barlow, Max G. *From The Shepherd's Purse*.
*Jensen, Bernard, D.C. *The Science and Practice of Iridology*.
*Christopher, Dr. John R. *The School of Natural Healing*. 1976.
Course Provided by National Iridology Association. 3930 East First
    Street: Tulsa, Oklahoma 74135.
Iridology Simplified. Contact Bernard Jensen. D.C., Route 1, Box
    52, Escondidio, California 92025.

HOMEOPATHY

Vithoulkas, George. *Homeopathy—Medicine For The New Man*.
Panos, Maesimund, M.D. and Heimlich, Jane. *Homeopathic
    Medicine at Home*.
Vithoulkas, George. *The Science of Homeopathy—A Modern Text
    Book*.

Whitmont, Edward, M.D. *Psyche and Substance—Essays in Homeopathy in light of Jun Gian, psychologist.*

Boericke, William, M.D. *Materia Medica With Repertory.*

All of the above books and many more are available from the Homeopathic Educatonal Services, 5916 Chabot Crest, Oakland, California 94618.

BIOLOGIC ENERGY AND ECOLOGY:

Long, Max Freedom. *Psychometric Analysis.* Santa Monica: Devorss, 1959.

Westlake, Aubrey T. *The Patterns of Health: Search for Greater Understanding of The Life Force in Health and Disease.* Berkley Shambhala Publications, 1961.

Pearce, Joseph Shulton. *The Crack in The Cosmic Egg.* New York: Pocketbook, 1973.

The Association For Research and Enlightenment. *A Search for God*, Book 1 and 2, 1942.

Incorporated, Virginia Beach, Virginia. Numerous other publications of interest are available through this organization.

Sperry, Robert M. *The Joy of Healing.* P.O. Box 25616, Seattle, Washington, 98125: Vulcan Books, 1978.

Verner, Fritz. *Electro-Acupuncture Primer.* Medizinisch Literarische Verlags Gesellschaft MBH, Ueozen.

Hill, Christopoher. *Supersensonics.* P.O. Box 644, Boulder Creek, California 95006: University of Trees Press.

Hill, Christopher. *Nuclear Evolution.* P.O. Box 644 Boulder Creek, California 95006: University of Trees Press. Numerous other books from the same source are recommended.

Oyle, Dr. Irving. *Time, Space and The Mind.* Millbrae, California: published by Celestial Arts, 1976.

Krieger, Dolores. Ph.D., R.N. *The Therapeutic Touch.* Englewood Cliffs, New Jersey 07632: Prentice Hall Inc., 1979.

Nixon, Frances. *Born to be Magnetic*. P.O. Box 718, Chemainus, British Columbia, Canada: Magnetic Publishers, Volume 1 and 2, 1971.

Tansley, David V. D.C. *Radionics and The Subtle Anatomy of Man*. Bradford, Holsworthy, Devon, England: Health Science Press.

Davis, Albert Roy. *The Anatomy of Biomagnetism*. Communicate at 520 Magnolia Avenue, Green Cove Springs, Florida 32043: 1974. Numerous other books by the same author are recommended as well.

Edited by Krippner, Stanley and Reuben, Daniel. *The Kirlian Aura: Photographing The Galaxies of Life*. Garden City, New York: Anchor Books, Anchor Press, Doubleday, 1974.

Ornstein, Robert E. *The Psychology of Consciousness*. New York: Harcourt, Brace and Jovanovich, 1977.

Laurie, Sanders G. and Tucker, Melvin, J., Ph.D. *Centering: Your Guide to Inner Growth*. A Warner Destiny Book, 1978.

Zamm, Alfred V., M.D., *Why Your House May Endanger Your Health*. Simon and Schuster, New York, 1980.

Golus, Natalie and Golbitz, Frances Golus. *Coping With Your Allergies*. Published by Simon and Schuster, New York, 1979.

Mackarness, Richard. *Eating Dangerously*. New York and London: Harcourt, Brace and Jovanovich, 1976.

Mandell, Dr. Marshall. *Five Day Relief System*. T. Y. Crowell, 1979.
Edited by Dickey, Lawrence D., M.D. *Clinical Ecology*. Springfield, Illinios: Charles C. Thomas Publishers, 1976.

KINESIOLOGY: (MUSCLE TESTING)

Diamond, Dr. John. *Your Body Doesn't Lie*. Warner Books, 1979.
Thie, John F., D.C., with Marks, Mary. *Touch For Health*. 1641 Lincoln Boulevard, Santa Monica, California 90404: DeVorss and Company, 1973.
Communicate with Goodhart, G. J., D.C. *Various Workshop Procedure Manuals of Applied Kinesiology*. 542 Michigan Boulevard, Detroit Michigan 48226: Specify what volume and year you wish.
A Division of the Institute of Behavioral Kinesiology. *Numerous publications by Dr. John Diamond for physicians*. P.O. Box Drawer 37, Valley Cottage, New York: published by Archaeus Press.

The Academy of Applied Osteopathy. *An Endocrine Interpretation of Chapman's Reflexes*. P.O. Box 1050, Carmel, California.

Pottenger, Frances M. Selected chapters from *Symptoms of Visceral Disease*. Available through the Academy of Applied Osteopathy.

Walther, David S., D.C., *Applied Kinesiology*. Systems, D.D., 275 West Abriendo, Pueblo, Colorado 81004: 1976.

Schmitt, Walter H. Jr., D.C., *Common Glandular Dysfunctions in The General Practice and Applied Kinesiologic Approach*. Applied Kinesiology Study Program, 1926 Overland Drive, Chappel Hill, North California 27514: 1981.

Eversaul, George A. *Dental Kinesiology*. All inquiries should be addressed to P.O. Box 19476, Las Vegas, Nevada 89119.

GENERAL RECOMMENDED READING:

Mannenberg, Don, M.D. and Roth, June. *Aerobic Nutrition*. 2 Park Avenue, New York, New York 10016: Elsevier-Dutton Publishing Company Incorporated, 1981.

Calella, John R. *Cooking Naturally*. Berkley California: AND/OR Press, 1978.

Mac Neil, Karen. *The Book of Whole Foods: Nutrition and Cuisine*. A division of Random House, New York: Vintage Books, 1981.

Kaslow, Arthur L. M.D., and Miles, Richard B. *You Can Achieve Freedom From Chronic Disease*. Los Angeles, California: J.P. Tarcher Incorporated, 1979.

Airola, Paavo. *How To Get Well*. Phoenix, Arizona: Health Plus Publishers. 1974.

Walker, Dr. Morton. *How Not To Have A Heart Attack*. A division of Franklin Watts, New York, New York: New Viewpoints/Vision Books, 1980.

McGee, Charles. *How To Survive Modern Technology*. P.O. Box 694, Alamo, California 94507: copyright 1979, published by Ecology Press.

Jensen, Bernard. D.C. *Doctor-Patient Handbook*. 1976. Route 1, Box 52, Escondido, Calfornia 92025: published by Bernard Jensen Enterprises, Fourth Printing 1981.

Brennan, Dr. R.O. *Nutra-Genetics*. E.M. Evans and Company Incorporated, New York, New York, 1975.

These are only a few of the books that have guided me on the path of producing this book. It would be impossible to list them all. However, we must remember that the essence of wisdom comes from within our minds and bodies and not from books.

Iridology Chart

Donald R. Bamer B.S.D.C.

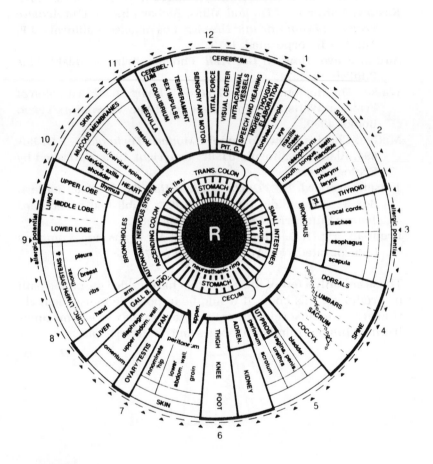

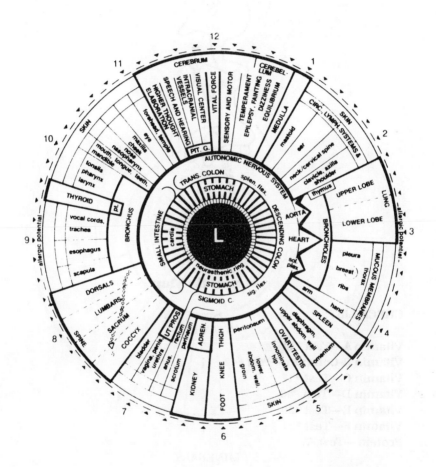

© 1979
DONALD R. BAMER B.S. D.C.

Magnetic Map

CHECK LIST:

VITAMINS

Vitamin A—Test #41
Vitamin B-Complex—Test #42
Vitamin C—Test #17
Vitamin D—Test #40
Vitamin E—Test #20
Vitamin F—Test #21
Protein—Test #3

MINERALS

Bioflavonoids—Test #18
Calcium—Test #19
Magnesium—Test #34
Manganese (Thymus)—Test #31
Sodium—Test #12
Potassium—Test #11

Iron—Test #40
Iodine—Test #16

GLANDS

Hypothalamus—Test #4
Pituitary—Test #5
Thyroid—Test #15
Adrenal—Test #30
Testes—Test #37
Ovaries—Test #35

DIGESTIVE TRACT

Parotid—Test #10
Liver—Test #24
Bile—Test #25
Pancreas—Test #33, #13
Stomach Acid—Test #26
GE Area—Test #27
Small Bowel—Test #39

Large Bowel (Sigmoid)—Test #39
Colon Valve—Test #32
Acidophilus—Test #22

OTHERS

Lungs—Test #23
Blood vessel instability—Test #38

CIRCUITS

HEAD:
Upper Cranial (Skull)—Test #6
Lower Cranial (Skull)—Test #7
TMJK (Temporomandibular Joint)—Test #8
Main Switch circuit—Test #1
Brain Dominance—Test #2
Jaw—Test #9
Sinus—Test #13

RESISTANCE

Lymph nodes—Test #14
Spleen—Test #28
Thymus—Test #31

URINARY

Bladder—Test #36
Kidney—Test #29

Some Manufacturers of Protomorphogens

(Glandular Products)

Standard Process Laboratories, 9103 Highway 67 South, Dallas, Texas 75211.

Sivad Bioresearch Company, 28003 John R. Street, Madison Heights, Michigan 48071

Seroyal, P.O. Box 36087, Houston, Texas 77036

Lanpar Company, 7101 Carpenter Freeway, Dallas, Texas 75247

V.M. Nutri-Food Distributors, Box 1298, Douglas, Wyoming 82633

Nutridine, P.O. Box 35329, Dallas, Texas 75235

Search, P.O. Box 35329, Dallas, Texas 75235

Carlson Division of J.R. Carlson Laboratories, Inc., Arlington Hts., IL 60004

Klaire Laboratories, Inc., P.O. Box 618, Carlsbad, CA. 92008

To The Physician

When I first saw this phenomenon in a demonstration, I rejected its existence and made no effort to reproduce any portion of the subject. Fortunately, I felt that two aspects of my total experience allowed me, many months later, to pursue the subject—curiosity and medical experience, what allows one to gain medical experience: time, training, successes and mistakes.

I was trained as a regular doctor and practiced long enough for some maturity to develop in my practice and philosophy.

As time went by, it became more evident that in spite of all our skills and knowledge, in spite of our continuing medical advances, we as physicians were inadequately coping with a large segment of our practice: Emotional problems were rampant and were not encountered realistically: nutritional abuses were common, allergic problems prevailed, and degenerative diseases offered bitter therapeutic opposition.

The usual data base of the history/physical, blood tests and X-rays allowed one to tell traditionally that he was doing "all one could do". In most cases, however, we obtained an inadequate data base. In effect, no significant environmental, nutritional, emotional or occupational history was obtained.

My experience convinced me that these areas were crucial enough to be evaluated in the general medical population by the general internist or family practitioner.

In addition to reorganizing my verbal and nonverbal data base, I then redirected my attention to the concept that perhaps the body, with its most intricate of all computers—the brain, may have a system of informing us what it prefers and what it rejects. Thus, with neither elation nor extreme skepticism, I studied basic Applied Kinesiology. It seemed unscientific, illogical and after first rejecting it, I decided to try it with some of my liberal patients. With a little practice, the system proved to be fantastically reproducible and effective as a diagnostic tool. Though nonspecific, I found I could integrate it rapidly into my existent data base. The danger of relying on biomagnetic testing as some semi-religious experience or as a solitary data base did not happen with me, though I can picture this happening with some physicians who may be anti-traditional and bitter about existent data methods.

I used the muscle testing to augment my physical examination only, and over several years this method was developed into the present system which takes less than four minutes to totally perform after practice. This system has little good scientific data to substantiate it and, thus, a portion of the physician readers who are comfortable with their present systems approach, will not pursue an objective evaluation of biomagnetics. One hundred or so years from now, we physicians will look back at our present system of healing with some admonition and an occasional snicker, and should approach the subject with objectivity.

There is much yet, that the basic scientist needs to document. The life force cannot be measured. Body energies have been recorded electrically by Hall at Yale in the '30's. Anyone with skill in acupuncture has an appreciation of such energy.

This evaluation as presented is best done by an interested and objective, open-minded (if you will), physician. He may then either utilize the nutritional and preventive methods found to be clinically repeatedly helpful, or may only use the information for record keeping in case the organ illness progresses and at a later stage, the more acceptable organ or blood tests become positive.

I believe that these energy factors reveal themselves before,

during and many times after the more traditional tests area changed and return to normal.

In no way is there an implication that this method of testing is to be substituted for any other currently used. It merely augments and gives nonspecific but reproducible and very sensitive information. I have purposely omitted certain reflexes such as heart, because they are not as heavily re-verifiable in my practice with this system and may give misleading information. More advanced energy methods, however, do correlate nicely in these areas. Other organs were not included in being tested because they do not easily apply to this system or because it would increase the complexity of the system so that it could not be grasped effectively.

To reduce bias, I do not explain or preliminarily discuss this test with an average patient. At times, I may sense that the personality of the patient is not suited for the testing, but usually we do it in the midst of other physical tests. I explain that I am testing muscle strength and simply testing some magnetic reflexes. If they remain curious, I explain that the body is electrical and around any element of electricity is a magnetic current. If the hand and fingers are magnetic as well as the body, then we have learned a few areas where the circuit can be closed and information can be obtained.

A patient will usually understand or accept this information.

The testing not only proves that the reflex is reproducibly abnormal, but there are other clinical advantages to this method of testing: (a) The patient feels a sense of participation in a patient/physician team approach. (b) The patient feels that you are willing to believe his *body*, to some extent, especially since the testing is generally not majorly influenced by the patient's belief or prejudicial system. (c) The physician is actually touching the patient—something lacking in our dehumanizing system of medicine.

As some physicians have an omnipotent attitude and feel uncomfortable having a team approach to life-style problem-solving with their patients, they will not be interested in this book. For those who are willing to pursue new ideas and frontiers, however, I wish you good success.

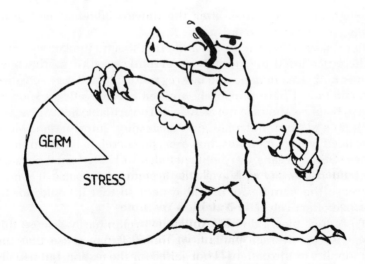

A Small part of a Big Picture

A home study course is available through:

Bio-Nutrition Institute
2537 Nottingham
Grand Prairie, TX 75050
(214) 647-1991

INDEX